As one of the world's longest established
and best-known travel brands,
Thomas Cook are the experts in travel.

For more than 135 years our
guidebooks have unlocked the secrets
of destinations around the world,
sharing vellers a wealth of
passion for travel.

as Cook as your
your next trip
ique heritage.

Thomas Cook **pocket** guides

TEL AVIV

Written by Samantha Wilson

Published by Thomas Cook Publishing
A division of Thomas Cook Tour Operations Limited
Company registration no. 3772199 England
The Thomas Cook Business Park, Unit 9, Coningsby Road,
Peterborough PE3 8SB, United Kingdom
Email: books@thomascook.com, Tel: +44 (0) 1733 416477
www.thomascookpublishing.com

Produced by Cambridge Publishing Management Limited
Burr Elm Court, Main Street, Caldecote CB23 7NU
www.cambridgepm.co.uk

ISBN: 978-1-84848-480-1

First edition © 2011 Thomas Cook Publishing
Text © Thomas Cook Publishing
Maps © Thomas Cook Publishing/PCGraphics (UK) Limited

Series Editor: Karen Beaulah
Production/DTP: Steven Collins

Printed and bound in Spain by GraphyCems

Cover photography © Eddie Gerald/Alamy

CONTENTS

SYMBOLS KEY

The following symbols are used throughout this book:

🅐 address 🕾 telephone 🅦 website address 🅔 email
🕓 opening times 🅝 public transport connections 🅘 important

The following symbols are used on the maps:

🅲 information office		▪ point of interest
✈ airport		○ city
➕ hospital		○ large town
🛡 police station		○ small town
🚍 bus station		＝ motorway
🚆 railway station		— main road
✝ cathedral		minor road
➊ numbers denote featured		— railway
cafés & restaurants		

Hotels and restaurants are graded by approximate price as follows:

£ budget price ££ mid-range price £££ expensive

 Tel Aviv's modern high-rises look down on the Mediterranean coastline

INTRODUCING
Tel Aviv

Introduction

To the unacquainted, Israel conjures up images of historic buildings, cobbled streets and devoutly religious inhabitants. While this may very well be the case across much of the country, for Tel Aviv it couldn't be further from the truth. Jerusalem may form Israel's spiritual core, but Tel Aviv revels in its role as the country's financial, fashion, culinary, art and nightlife capital. It is a young, vibrant and secular Mediterranean city, based around its beach and the café-lined boulevards that are packed at all hours. The 24-hour nightlife is legendary, its art galleries world famous and its restaurants first rate.

Tel Aviv is a new city in a land of ancient ones. Founded by Jewish Zionists who left Jaffa a century ago, it has played a crucial role in Israel's development – from being the signing-place of the declaration of independence to playing home to the country's embassies and consulates. It shares the job of capital with Jerusalem – the latter not recognised as such by much of the international community. It is the financial, economic and administrative centre; a place where a prosperous diamond exchange, a seafront lined with five-star hotels and the biggest business space in the Middle East can be found.

Yet the city is so much more than all business. Bars and clubs stay open until the small hours even mid-week, and the restaurant scene has caught the interest of international food connoisseurs. Neighbourhood galleries showcasing the works of local and international artists are now an essential stop for curators from around the world, and theatre, opera, ballet and music all thrive.

Tel Aviv's residents are incredibly proud of their city, and enjoy it to its fullest. Few would describe the place as beautiful – its Bauhaus architecture and its status as a UNESCO World Heritage Site notwithstanding – and it doesn't profess to be. Its charm lies most evidently in its fun, vibrant atmosphere, where anything goes, and *joie de vivre* and *lechaim* (cheers) seem to be the motto.

⬤ *A streetside fresh-juice bar provides tasty refreshments*

When to go

Tel Aviv's consistently warm climate makes visiting possible at any time of year. The summer months of June to August are extremely hot, which means sightseeing can be sweaty and uncomfortable, especially during the middle of the day. But if you're after a beach, balmy summer evening parties and sipping lattes in cool cafés then this is when to go. Prices for hotels and flights do tend to soar at this time, however, which, combined with the sweltering weather, mean spring or autumn may be a better bet. These seasons are ideal for wandering around the city's neighbourhoods, enigmatic markets and lively boulevards, with the sun shining but temperatures slightly milder and a breeze blowing off the sea. Winter months can see rain and, while Tel Aviv doesn't experience temperatures anywhere near as cold as Jerusalem, it can get chilly at night.

SEASONS & CLIMATE

Tel Aviv has a Mediterranean climate with two distinct seasons. At the height of summer Tel Aviv's temperatures can easily reach 30°C (86°F), which, combined with intense humidity, make air conditioning a highly appreciated commodity. Summers are dry and any rainfall whatsoever outside of the winter months is pretty much unknown. Altogether, this region receives approximately 500 mm (20 in) of rain annually, by far the greater amount falling between December and February. Bright, sunny days are a common event throughout winter as well, and rainfall is concentrated into only a few days (on average 44 per year). Temperatures hover around 12°C (54°F) in the day but can get as

The annual Gay Pride celebration is always a colourful event

low as 6°C (43°F) so be sure to pack your winter coat. The spring and autumn months are milder and less humid than July and August, with daytime temperatures averaging 22°C (72°F).

ANNUAL EVENTS
February–March
Purim This is one of Judaism's happiest and liveliest holidays. Fancy dress is donned by all and the bars and pubs are full to bursting for a night of lively frivolity. It usually falls in March.

April–May
Holocaust Memorial Day A sombre and emotional day of remembrance for the six million Jews who lost their lives in this terrible genocide. It is commemorated with a public holiday, whereon a quiet air of reflection and sadness permeates the usually bustling city.

War Memorial Day Held one week after Holocaust Memorial Day, it commemorates the fallen soldiers of Israel's wars. It is a painful and sad day in a country where everyone knows someone who has lost a loved one in the name of duty.

Independence Day At the close of War Memorial Day the country erupts into vibrant festivities in celebration of their declaration of independence. Street parties are held throughout the country. In Tel Aviv the biggest party is in Rabin Square.

Taste of the City The city's world-class restaurants showcase their finest dishes in the HaYarkon Exhibition Centre in May. Gourmet taster dishes can be bought for 20NIS and it is a great way to savour Tel Aviv's culinary prowess.

June

Gay Pride Tel Aviv shows off its liberal, secular colours in a fun, happy parade through the city's streets that takes place in June. Beginning at Rabin Square it heads slowly through the throngs of spectators and partygoers to HaYarkon Park.

November

Tel Aviv Spirit Film Festival Hard-hitting, thought-provoking films (in English and Hebrew) are screened at the Tel Aviv Cinematheque in this four-day-long festival in November.
ⓦ www.spiritfestival.co.il

PUBLIC HOLIDAYS

Pesach (Passover) 7–14 Apr 2012, 25 Mar–2 Apr 2013
Holocaust Memorial Day 19 Apr 2012, 8 Apr 2013
War Memorial Day 25 Apr 2012, 15 Apr 2013
Independence Day 26 Apr 2012, 16 Apr 2013
Shavuot (Pentecost) 27 May 2012, 15 May 2013
Rosh Hashana 29–30 Sept 2011, 17–18 Sept 2012, 5–6 Sept 2013
Yom Kippur (Day of Atonement) 8 Oct 2011, 26 Sept 2012, 14 Sept 2013
Sukkot (Feast of Tabernacles) 19 Oct 2011, 1 Oct 2012, 19 Sept 2013
Hannukah 21–28 Dec 2011, 9–15 Dec 2012, 28 Nov–5 Dec 2013

Yom Kippur

Yom Kippur in Tel Aviv is a day like no other: not a single car drives down the normally bumper-to-bumper streets, children ride bicycles along the great motorways, the sound of waves lapping at the sea's edge can be heard from blocks away, and the city's usually busy, industrious residents sit quietly indoors or lounge in the parks.

Yom Kippur is the holiest day in Judaism, a quiet day which Jews spend atoning for their sins of the past year, through prayer and self-denial, and thinking about the year to come. Even normally non-conformist Jews will visit the synagogue and fast for 25 hours (from sunset to sunset) – an act considered to aid the cleansing of the soul. The Day of Atonement, as it is known, is a day of repentance and reflection, and even in this most secular of cities, it is a spiritually important day in the lives of its residents.

Spending the day in Tel Aviv on Yom Kippur feels like stepping onto the set of an apocalypse-themed film. The streets, void of traffic and crowds, are at the same time eerie and amazing, with not a single business opening its doors. Being able to hear the gentle sounds usually blocked out by the urban din, wander down the middle of a normally busy junction or do absolutely nothing for an entire day is a uniquely Israeli experience.

For despite its secular, fun-loving attitude Tel Aviv is just as passionate about Yom Kippur as its more religious counterparts. While the profound religious sentiment may not be as strong as in Jerusalem (and many will rent films and spend the day eating), it is equally important in its own way. For this is a day when everything stops, when residents reflect on their lives and when the entire city takes a deep breath before tomorrow comes and busy lives resume once again.

🔺 *During Yom Kippur, the city's usually crowded highways are deserted*

History

Modern Tel Aviv is considered a youngster in this ancient country, its roots dating back only as far as 1910. Known officially as Tel Aviv-Jaffa, it was founded by several Jewish families who sought to create a new neighbourhood outside Jaffa (which, conversely, has one of the oldest histories in the country). The ancient southern suburb has played a crucial role in the shaping of the modern city.

Four-thousand-year-old Jaffa is one of the world's oldest continuously active ports. Whereas today small fishing boats chug in and out of a sleepy old harbour, this was once a major trading post, most notably throughout the Egyptian and Ottoman empires and after the opening of the Suez Canal in 1869, when ships and pilgrims poured into the Holy Land from all over Europe.

Jaffa's origins lie long before that, however, and the city is mentioned several times in biblical texts, not least as the port through which the wood for King Solomon's First Temple in Jerusalem arrived.

In 1099 Jaffa was conquered by the Crusaders, and Jerusalem's Great Trunk Road constructed. In 1268 Baibars, the Mamluk Sultan at the time, ousted the Crusaders, destroying Jaffa to prevent further Crusader incursions. A small population remained, but it wasn't until the Ottomans took control in the 16th century that it once again sprang to life. Despite a plague, and a siege by Napoleon, Jaffa quickly rebounded and over the 19th century it matured into an important urban centre. It was during this time of great population growth that the Jewish residents of Jaffa sought to found new neighbourhoods just to its north.

Jaffa flourished as a Palestinian city until the 1936–39 rebellions saw the port closed in favour of a new one in Tel Aviv. In 1948 Arab forces in Jaffa shelled nearby Tel Aviv; Jewish forces retaliated by capturing the Old City on 12 May 1948, two days before Israel went on to declare independence. After this, most of the 65,000 Palestinians left the city and in 1950 Jaffa was incorporated into the municipality of Tel Aviv.

Waves of Jewish immigration to the country saw the population boom and the modern city quickly develop. Finance, industry, Jewish culture and the arts all prospered, Bauhaus architecture appeared (see page 88), and the city hasn't looked back since. Throughout the last century Tel Aviv has become one of the most cosmopolitan, cultural and significant municipalities in the Middle East and, as the seat of Israel's embassies and financial sector, shares responsibilities with Jerusalem, which much of the international community refuses to recognise as the country's capital city.

● *Tel Aviv is closely associated with the distinctive Bauhaus style*

Lifestyle

Tel Aviv is a young, secular city with liberal, friendly residents. This is particularly evident in the abundance of cafés, bars and restaurants which are open straight through the religious Shabbat, or Sabbath, and of which few are kosher. In contrast to Jerusalem, when Friday evening sees the city quieten down, Tel

● *Tel Aviv's warm, sunny climate is well suited to surfing*

Aviv's busiest night out is Friday, with hard-working Tel Avivis filling the bars and nightclubs and really letting their hair down. 'Pick-up' bars (as they are known even to Hebrew-speaking locals) pump out the latest tunes while scantily clad partygoers flirt and dance the night away. Laid-back pubs, neighbourhood-style bars and late-night bohemian cafés all also play their part in entertaining the diverse population.

While this pricey city may appeal most obviously to those in their twenties or thirties who have cash to spend, its demographics are in fact wide-reaching. A stroll along the seafront promenade or through the Dizengoff Center will reveal young families, older residents, a large gay community, Orthodox Jews and ex-pats, all of whom also call Tel Aviv home.

The city is an informal one, where you will rarely see a man wearing a suit; wedding-attire is jeans and a shirt, and dress codes for bars are unheard of. That isn't to say that fashion doesn't play a huge role in the lifestyle of Tel Aviv's trendy residents. The sheer number of boutiques and shopping centres attests to this, but closer inspection will reveal that casual chic is the theme. Looking good but not appearing to have made much of an effort seems to be the trend.

The working week runs from Sunday to Friday afternoon, although many offices are closed throughout Friday and Saturday. Jewish Shabbat begins at sunset on Friday and runs until sunset on Saturday. Public transport doesn't run during this time and many museums, galleries and most shops will be closed, reopening on Saturday evening. Friday is the day to lounge around in cafés, go shopping and get ready for a big night out, while Saturday tends to be more relaxed, with trips to the beach and family time a priority.

Culture

Since before Israel's declaration of independence, Tel Aviv has been a centre of culture and the arts, which today form such an important and prevalent component of city life. From its designation as a UNESCO World Heritage Site, to its abundance of Bauhaus architecture, to boasting a world-class art museum and a renowned philharmonic orchestra, Tel Aviv is Israel's cultural hub.

The Tel Aviv Museum of Art (see page 71) is outstanding, but it is far from being the only art museum in the city. Indeed, art plays a huge role in the cultural scene and is encouraged wholeheartedly across the municipality. Areas such as Jaffa (see page 94), Neve Tzedek (see page 85) and Florentine have emerged as artistic centres, each with dozens of workshops and galleries in which works by renowned and up-and-coming local artists are put on show.

Boutique hotels displaying pieces by local artists further exemplify Tel Aviv's artistic side, while the twice-weekly Nachalat Binyamin Craft Market (see page 90) is a colourful outdoor fair for artists to exhibit their works.

Jerusalem certainly takes the museum crown, being home to the Yad Vashem Holocaust Memorial Museum and the Israel Museum (see page 112), but Tel Aviv has its own wealth of interesting museums, most focusing on the history and culture of the Jewish people. Restored houses of prominent Jewish politicians and poets, as well as sprawling pavilions housing a plethora of ethnographic, cultural, religious and historical artefacts, take Zionism and the Jewish homeland's eventual creation as predominant themes.

Hebrew theatre is a thriving art, at the pinnacle of which sits the national Habima Theatre (see page 68), whose sell-out performances and full-time troupe attest to its popularity in

🔺 *The historic port of Jaffa*

mainstream society. Smaller theatres also put on regular shows – most of which are in Hebrew (the Habima Theatre does offer simultaneous English translation).

Dance has not, until recently, held the same status as theatre or music. However, thanks largely to the Suzanne Dellal Dance Academy in Neve Tzedek, which is home to the Bat Sheva modern dance troupe and puts on a variety of ballet, jazz and folk-dance performances, it is today rapidly increasing in esteem and popularity.

The Mann Auditorium (see page 70) is home to the Israel Philharmonic, the country's most acclaimed and internationally respected orchestra. It plays to sell-out audiences and hosts guest conductors from around the world. The New Israeli Opera has also seen massive success in recent years and puts on regular performances in the city.

Music in general plays a big role in Tel Avivian (and indeed Israeli) society, and spans all musical styles from classical and opera to jazz to mainstream pop and the ever-popular techno.

 Nachalat Binyamin Craft Market offers a great selection of souvenirs

MAKING THE MOST OF

Tel Aviv

Shopping

Tel Aviv is the country's retail-therapy hub and Israelis love nothing more than ambling along its shop-lined streets, exploring the vast shopping centres and haggling at the open-air markets. Boutiques, antiques, high-street shops, souvenirs, gaudy wedding dresses, shoes galore, jewellery, Judaica, arts and crafts, furniture and fresh produce all have their own place and can all be found in abundance, although prices are higher than in most European countries.

Visitors to the Middle East come expecting bustling open-air markets filled with the scents of spices, fresh fruit and sweet desserts – and Tel Aviv doesn't disappoint. In the midst of the busy cosmopolitan city is HaCarmel Market (see page 82), a long narrow pedestrian street crammed with stalls selling everything from confectionery to household items to discounted Dead Sea products (which make great souvenirs) to fresh meats, dairy, fruit and vegetables. Adjacent to the top entrance of the market is the Nachalat Binyamin Craft Market (see page 90), a popular and lively twice-weekly event showcasing some of the city's finest artists and their unusual crafts. The old Jaffa flea market is today one of the trendiest up-and-coming areas, not only for scouting out antiques, bric-a-brac and collectibles, but also for enjoying a coffee, meal or evening drink. It epitomises bohemian chic, a trend that is coming to define Tel Aviv.

Israelis love shopping centres and Tel Aviv is home to several, including the country's first – the 1980s-style Dizengoff Center. Holding pride of place in the heart of the city, it is a maze of mainstream shops and cafés, and includes a cinema complex, supermarket and, come Friday morning, a popular food fair. The towering Azrieli buildings are also home to a slightly more upmarket shopping centre, where designer outlets can be found, while the small but plush Opera Tower Shopping Centre on the seafront also offers higher priced items.

One of the best things about Tel Aviv's shopping scene is its surplus of unique, one-of-a-kind boutiques. While high-street shops such as Castro and Fox have their popular place, it is the quirky clothes and shoe boutiques that line streets such as Sheinkin, Dizengoff and Allenby or those in neighbourhoods such as the Electric Garden and Nachalat Binyamin that really give Tel Aviv its shopping flair.

🔵 *Seek out a bargain at Nachalat Binyamin Craft Market*

Eating & drinking

Tel Aviv's biggest selling point is perhaps its cuisine. Israeli social life centres around food, whether it's a romantic meal for two, a late-night bar snack with friends or a hummus brunch catch-up. And in this young, vibrant and affluent city, there is no shortage of fabulous places to enjoy a bite to eat.

The best and most noticeable thing about food in Tel Aviv is the sheer variety of culinary styles present. Waves of immigrants from around the world have seen every style and tradition of food incorporated into mainstream eating, and while hummus and falafel are still the number-one quick eats, everything from South American steakhouses to noodle and sushi bars, from fish and seafood to vegetarian dishes can be found.

Unlike Jerusalem, few restaurants in Tel Aviv are kosher (although pork is still notably rare on menus), and while its Holy City counterparts mostly close for Shabbat, Tel Aviv's restaurants fling open their doors.

RESTAURANTS

Tel Aviv has some of the most highly acclaimed restaurants in the world, and its high-end gourmet establishments are famous for their Mediterranean-fusion cuisine. The good news for visitors without bottomless pockets is that the range of restaurants is very wide and so it is easy to find something to suit every budget. Good quality can be expected; Israelis have hugely high standards and anything not up to par simply won't survive. Restaurants tend to have a short shelf-life in this fast-paced city and what is the hottest place today may be long-forgotten tomorrow – look for queues down the street denoting the current 'in' spot.

CAFÉS

Café culture has come to define the city, and there is nothing more Tel Avivian than sipping a perfectly blended latte in one of the pavement-lining cafés. Ranging from the super-chic to the bohemian, from quiet to bustling, and from organic vegetarian to chain brands there is something to suit every caffeinated taste. In addition to superb coffee (Israelis are very particular), a variety of teas, smoothies and fruit juices can always be found, and most cafés have extensive and creative menus. An enormous breakfast of eggs, salads, breads, olives and cheeses is a great way to start the day.

FAST FOOD ISRAELI-STYLE

Hummus and falafel are the jewels of Israel's quick-eats crown, and while the unaccustomed digestive system may initially balk at too many chickpeas, you soon habituate yourself to it. Cheap, quick and downright delicious, these fast foods sustain the

PRICE CATEGORIES
The restaurant price guides used in this book indicate the approximate cost of a three-course meal for one person, excluding drinks, at the time of writing.
£ up to 40NIS ££ 40–70NIS £££ over 70NIS

● *Busy outdoor cafés line Sheinkin Street*

population's savoury cravings and make a great lunch or mid-afternoon snack.

Hummus is mashed chickpeas blended with tahini (sesame) sauce and eaten sopped up with big chunks of warm pitta bread. Falafel consists of balls of chickpeas, herbs and spices deep fried and served in pitta with a variety of salads and sauces. A popular variation on this is *sabich*, which replaces the falafel balls with hard-boiled eggs and fried aubergine.

In addition to hummus and falafel, there is a whole host of tasty street snacks around – *shawarma* (thinly sliced lamb served in pitta), *burekas* (stuffed pastry parcels), Italian ice-cream parlours, juice bars and doorstop sandwiches are all affordable and widespread.

TIPPING & ETIQUETTE

Despite often-questionable service, Israelis are big tippers, and 12 per cent is customary. Service has improved in recent years, but surly or snooty waiting staff are still a force to be reckoned with.

Israelis eat late and like to linger over a meal, and while most restaurants open for the evening at around 18.00 you can expect to be the only patron until at least 20.00 or 21.00. Indeed, most establishments stay open late, and bars (see page 28) will serve high-quality snacks and light bites for as long as they are open.

Entertainment & nightlife

Tel Aviv is incredibly proud of its status as the Middle East's party city. Its young, vivacious residents love nothing more than letting their hair down on weekends when the bars, nightclubs and restaurants are full to bursting. The city is also the hub of Israel's cultural scene (see pages 18–19), with theatre, music, ballet, opera and cinema all thriving.

BARS & NIGHTCLUBS

From the 'pick-up' bars where scantily clad twenty-somethings flirt away in loud glitzy haunts, to the ultra-trendy wine bars, to gay and lesbian bars and casual neighbourhood-style pubs, Tel Aviv has something to suit every after-dark taste. Yet individual bars don't tend to stick around too long – what is popular today will likely have been replaced a year on in this fast-paced city where fashion is a lifestyle.

There are several main clusters of places to drink in Tel Aviv. Dizengoff Street and the boulevards leading off it are home to plenty of mainstream watering holes, while chic wine bars can be found along Rothschild Boulevard (see page 85). The renovated old port in the north is a heavyweight night-time hotspot, full of large bars with dance floors and trance and hard rock nightclubs. The funky, artistic neighbourhoods of Florentine, Neve Tzedek and Levontine attract a more laid-back set. The flea market in Jaffa (see page 98) is also one of the most up-and-coming 'in' places to be seen, with its bohemian vibe and host of chilled late-night bars and cafés (see page 103).

CONCERTS

Israelis are delighted that their country is increasingly being included on the tours of many international artists, who often now perform in HaYarkon Park. Posters appear all over Tel Aviv well in advance of major concerts, which are also listed in English-language publications such as *Haaretz*, the *Jerusalem Post* (English daily newspapers) and *Time Out Israel*. Tickets can be purchased via a central toll-free number.

Classical concerts are also sell-outs, and getting tickets to see the Israel Philharmonic Orchestra at the Mann Auditorium (see page 70) is sometimes difficult. Tickets can be bought from the auditorium office or at the box offices on page 31.

● *Hanging out in the laid-back neighbourhood of Neve Tzedek*

The Rav Hen cinema at Dizengoff Square

Hadran @ 90 Ibn Gvirol St ☎ 03 5279797 ⓦ www.hadran.co.il
Kastel @ 153 Ibn Gvirol St ☎ 03 6045000 ⓦ www.tkts.co.il
Lean @ 101 Dizengoff St ☎ 03 5247373 ⓦ www.leaan.co.il

THEATRE & DANCE

The Habima Theatre (see page 68) may be the city's theatrical focal point but the city has more than a dozen additional smaller theatres, most of which put on performances in Hebrew, with the occasional English-language show. Tickets for these as well as for the Israel Ballet, modern-dance performances, New Israel Opera and countless smaller acts can be bought from the box offices (see above) or, in the case of the New Israel Opera (which is in season in autumn and winter), from the **Tel Aviv Performing Arts Center** (@ 19 Shaul Hamelech Blvd ☎ 03 6927777 ⓦ www.israel-opera.co.il).

CINEMA

The Tel Aviv Cinematheque (see page 71) broadcasts an arty selection of films in English or Hebrew with subtitles. Tickets can be bought from the box office outside. For mainstream flicks, which are shown in their original language – usually English – and subtitled in Hebrew, try the **Lev Cinema** (@ Ground Floor, Dizengoff Center ☎ 03 6200485 ❶ Admission charge) or the **Rav Hen Movie Theatre** (@ Dizengoff Sq & Azrieli Towers ☎ 03 5282288 ❶ Admission charge).

Sport & relaxation

SPECTATOR SPORTS

The **Nokia Stadium** (ⓐ 51 Yigal Alon St ⓣ 03 5376376
ⓦ www.sportpalace.co.il) in southeast Tel Aviv is the home of
Maccabi Tel Aviv, the city's beloved and very successful
basketball team. The **Bloomfield Stadium** (ⓐ Between Ha-Thiya
and She'erit Israel Streets ⓣ 03 6376000 ⓦ www.sportpalace.
co.il) in the south is the home of Hapoel Tel Aviv and Maccabi Tel
Aviv football clubs.

The Maccabiah Games are held every four years in Israel,
with many events taking place in Tel Aviv and Jewish athletes
from around the world competing. The last event was in 2009
and attracted over 6,000 athletes.

ⓐ *Beach volleyball is a popular Tel Avivian pastime*

RECREATIONAL SPORTS

Tel Aviv's warm, sunny climate lends itself to popular outdoor activities year round. You will find locals biking, jogging along the seafront, partaking in early-morning yoga on the beach, playing bat and ball or beach volleyball, scuba diving, swimming and windsurfing.

HaYarkon Park (see page 62) is also a popular area for recreational activities, boasting a boating lake, free volleyball, basketball and table-tennis facilities and a cycle path, which together attract scores of city-dwellers looking for some fresh air. There are many cycle paths across the city, although pedestrians do tend to walk on them, and bicycles can be rented all over (see page 56).

The outdoor **Gordon Swimming Pool** complex (ⓐ Gordon Beach ⓣ 03 /623300 ⓛ 06.00–21.00 Mon & Thur, 06.00–20.00 Tues & Wed, 06.00–19.00 Fri, 07.00 -18.00 Sat, 13.30–20.00 Sun ⓘ Admission charge) closed down in 2009 but was renovated and reopened due to popular demand and now offers refreshing Olympic-sized saltwater pools.

RELAXATION

Green spaces such as HaYarkon Park are popular spots where the whole family can join in a day of eating, chattering, playing Frisbee and relaxing.

As much as they like the outdoors, Israelis love to be pampered and Tel Aviv has undergone spa mania. All good hotels offer spa facilities. On the same theme is the craze for yoga that has taken hold of the city's residents, with classes easily arranged through hotels.

Accommodation

Tel Aviv is well equipped for visitors and is brimming with hotels of all shapes and sizes. Nonetheless, the Israel Ministry of Tourism has reported that there are still more wannabe visitors than hotel rooms and that, come the summer months, they are full to bursting. Because of this, or perhaps in spite of it, prices can be very steep. High-end and boutique hotels dominate the selection, but there is a growing number of budget hostels. Mid-range establishments are, however, still somewhat few and far between.

BUDGET HOTELS & HOSTELS

Tel Aviv's hostel and guesthouse scene is surprisingly good, from uncrowded dormitories with air conditioning to tidy double rooms with television and en-suite or shared facilities. Many also offer a whole host of other services and amenities including bicycle hire, communal kitchens, games rooms, barbecue areas and tour booking.

Florentine Hostel £ The Florentine neighbourhood in South Tel Aviv is one of the trendiest, most laid-back parts of the city, making this an ideal hostel location. It offers double rooms and dormitories and has an excellent range of facilities including Wi-Fi, a communal kitchen, laundry and mobile phone and bicycle hire. It operates an 18–40 age restriction.
ⓐ 10 Elifelet St ⓣ 03 5187551 ⓦ www.florentinehostel.com
ⓔ rafi@florentinehostel.com

Old Jaffa Hostel £ This hostel captures all the Jaffa charm, with rustic decoration and cosy rooms in a traditional stone building. To make it even better it is located near the flea market and has free Wi-Fi, laundry facilities and a communal kitchen for guests. ⓐ 8 Olei Zion St ⓣ 03 6822370 ⓦ www.telaviv-hostel.com ⓔ ojhostel@shani.net

Hayarkon 48 Hostel £–££ Two minutes from the beach and just off Allenby Street is this fantastic hostel that is fully geared towards independent travellers (and often fully booked). It has private rooms and dorm beds, a well-equipped communal kitchen, tons of facilities and a young, lively atmosphere. ⓐ 48 HaYarkon St ⓣ 03 5168989 ⓦ www.hayarkon48.com ⓔ info@hayarkon48.com

MID-RANGE HOTELS

Tel Aviv is unfortunately lacking in this type of accommodation, and finding a pleasant, affordable double room is increasingly difficult. They do of course exist, but will need to be booked much further in advance as they're highly sought-after. Mid-range hotels tend to be found in less central areas and away from the seafront. An en-suite bathroom, breakfast, Wi-Fi,

PRICE CATEGORIES
All prices are for one weekend night in a double or twin room, not including breakfast:
£ under 300NIS   ££ 300–600NIS   £££ over 600NIS

television and air conditioning should all come as standard, but do check out your options as a better deal and superior rooms can often be found in hostels and guesthouses.

Gordon Inn Hotel and Guesthouse £–££ While it may not look much from the outside, the rooms (with shared or en-suite bathroom) are pleasantly decorated, very clean and have TV, coffee facilities and Wi-Fi. There are also good-value dormitory beds. ⓐ 17 Gordon St ⓣ 03 5238239 ⓦ www.gordoninn.hostel. com ⓔ gordonin@gmail.com

Eden House ££ A lovely little guesthouse with spacious rooms, free Wi-Fi, shady outside areas and the touch of a family-run place. Rooms and self-catering apartments available. ⓐ 27 Kehilat Eden St ⓣ 052 7469842 ⓦ www.edenhousetlv.com ⓔ edenhousetlv@gmail.com

Maxim Hotel ££ This is one of the best value mid-range hotels around and has a great city-centre setting near the beach. Rooms are fairly small but very pleasant and are equipped with air conditioning, television and Wi-Fi. The hotel also offers room service and a breakfast buffet. ⓐ 86 HaYarkon St ⓣ 03 5173721 ⓦ www.maxim-htl-ta.co.il

Miguel Hotel and Bistro ££ With a central seaside location and lovely little bistro restaurant downstairs, Miguel's resembles the elegant, family-run hotels of France and Italy and has lots of character and finesse. Rooms are equipped with AC, TV and Wi-Fi. ⓐ 88 HaYarkon St ⓣ 03 5107744 ⓦ www.miguel.co.il

⬤ The distinctive Isrotel Tower offers luxury accommodation

HIGH-END HOTELS

Tel Aviv's shoreline is strewn with large four- and five-star hotel chains with first-rate amenities (although visitors often find the level of service lacking in comparison to Europe). Boutique hotels are the new super-trend and these small, luxurious hotels ooze personality and individuality, even if they sometimes err on the side of being pretentious. While the large high-end hotels tend to cluster along the seafront, boutique hotels can be found in a variety of different locales from central Dizengoff Square to neighbourhoods such as Neve Tzedek.

◐ *Neve Tzedek offers a range of accommodation types*

Center Hotel £££ This quirky hotel is housed within a Bauhaus building and each room is decorated differently with modern-art pieces by local artists. It has a great central location off Dizengoff Square. ⓐ 2 Zamenhof St ⓣ 03 5266100 ⓦ www.atlas.co.il ⓔ reservations@atlashotels.co.il

Hotel de la Mer £££ Feng shui principles have been used to design this chic, elegant boutique hotel and the result is a tranquil atmosphere, bright airy rooms with sea views and a top-notch spa. ⓐ 2 Nes Tziona St ⓣ 03 5100011 ⓦ www.delamer.co.il

Isrotel Tower £££ The towering circular hotel is an unmistakable landmark seen from across the city. It has a rooftop pool, beachside location and luxury amenities. ⓐ 78 HaYarkon St ⓣ 03 5113636 ⓦ www.isrotel.co.il

PRICES & BOOKING

There are ways to save a lot of money on high priced accommodation simply by timing your trip to avoid the most popular times of year and, where possible, weekends. Hotels are known to almost double their prices at the weekends, making city breaks much more affordable if you visit mid-week. Likewise, July and August are the peak holiday season, so visiting outside of these months is recommended. Availability also poses a problem in peak season so booking ahead is a must. In low and shoulder season, however, it is possible simply to show up, although this is uncommon.

THE BEST OF TEL AVIV

While Tel Aviv has some excellent attractions, the main appeal for visitors to the city is its charm and atmosphere, where sitting in a trendy café, ambling along the seafront promenade, dining in world-class restaurants or partying the night away are top of the list. That said, be sure to visit some of the city's great museums, peruse the traditional markets and soak up the charisma of the old neighbourhoods.

TOP 10 ATTRACTIONS

- **Rothschild Boulevard** Restaurants, cafés and Bauhaus architecture line Tel Aviv's most famous boulevard, where residents come to sip lattes, walk their dogs and listen to street musicians (see page 85).

- **Neve Tzedek neighbourhood** Tel Aviv's first neighbourhood is today a charismatic area with a bohemian, arty feel (see page 85).

- **Spend a day on the beach** Wide sandy beaches line the city's shoreline, which in the summer is the best place to cool off from the heat of the day (see page 58).

- **HaCarmel Market** The vibrant street market is a true Middle Eastern experience where everything is haggled for – from spices and olives to clothing and household items (see page 82).

- **Tel Aviv Museum of Art** The museum stands as the centrepiece of Israel's cultural scene and is one of the world's most highly acclaimed art museums (see page 71).

- **Spend Friday night on the town** Tel Aviv's party reputation comes alive on Friday night when young Tel Avivis hit the late-night bars, pubs and nightclubs (see page 28).

- **Eretz Israel Museum** The museum provides a fascinating insight into the history and culture of the Jewish people and the creation of the State of Israel (see page 68).

- **Sip coffee on Dizengoff Street** Pull up a chair in one of the many funky outdoor cafés that line Dizengoff Street for a spot of people-watching and a big Israeli breakfast (see page 74).

- **Jaffa Old City** Four-thousand-year-old Jaffa is steeped in old-world charm, with cobbled lanes, an artists' quarter, a quaint fishing port and a flea market (see page 94).

- **Sample the local cuisine** Lunch doesn't come better than a cheap, tasty and filling falafel bought freshly cooked from one of the many stands around the city (see page 25).

⬇ *The beach promenade is ideal for cycling*

Suggested itineraries

HALF-DAY: TEL AVIV IN A HURRY

Soak up the young cosmopolitan vibe, undoubtedly the essence and highlight of a trip to Tel Aviv. Walk down Rothschild Boulevard (see page 85), amble along the seafront promenade, sip coffee in one of Dizengoff's cafés and enjoy authentic falafel for lunch.

1 DAY: TIME TO SEE A LITTLE MORE

If you have the rest of the day at your disposal, work in a visit to HaCarmel Market (see page 82), Sheinkin Street (see page 86) and the Neve Tzedek neighbourhood (see page 85). Be sure also to spend a few hours in the cobbled lanes of Jaffa's Old City.

2–3 DAYS: TIME TO SEE MUCH MORE

Now you can really get to know Tel Aviv. Take your time over the sights and streets mentioned above, allowing for at least half a day exploring Jaffa's Old City, port, artists' quarter and flea market. Pay a visit to the Eretz Israel Museum (see page 68), visit Rabin Square (see page 62), browse the stalls of Nachalat Binyamin Craft Market (see page 90) and have a dip in the Mediterranean Sea. Spend an evening in the lively bars and restaurants of the restored port, catch a film at the Tel Aviv Cinematheque (see page 71) and take a walking tour of the city's striking Bauhaus architecture.

LONGER: ENJOYING TEL AVIV TO THE FULL

As above, plus spend an afternoon cycling through HaYarkon Park (see page 62), wander around the boutiques in the Electric

Garden and Yemenite Vineyard neighbourhoods (see pages 90 & 82). See a theatre or orchestra production, get a bird's-eye view from the Azrieli Observatory (see page 58), have coffee in the newly restored train station and visit Independence Hall (see page 86) and the Tel Aviv Museum of Art (see page 71). Factor in a full day trip to Jerusalem too, if time allows.

● Mix with the locals at Jaffa's flea market

Something for nothing

Tel Aviv's tourism board is fully embracing its new-found status as a top city-break destination, and is actively coming up with new ways for visitors to be entertained. Even better news is that there are some truly excellent experiences to be had for very little or no cost at all.

The wide, golden sandy beaches that fringe the city are free and have excellent facilities including lifeguards, bathroom and shower blocks, shaded areas, and cafés and restaurants. Join in a lively and competitive game of *matkot* (bat and ball), try your feet at dancing sessions or watch street performers on the promenade. The length of the promenade from HaYarkon Park to Jaffa also makes a lovely walk.

The Tel Aviv municipality, too, offers some worthwhile, free guided tours of the city. Choose from the **Tel Aviv: Art and Architecture tour** (ⓐ Dyonon bookstore, university campus entrance 🕐 11.00 Mon), the **Bauhaus: 'The White City' tour** (ⓐ 46 Rothschild Blvd 🕐 11.00 Sat), the **Tel Aviv by Night tour** (ⓐ Corner of Rothschild Blvd and Herzl St 🕐 20.00 Tues) or the **Old Jaffa tour** (ⓐ Clock Tower 🕐 09.30 Wed). In addition, there is a free downloadable MP3 walking tour downloadable from ⓦ www.visit-tlv.com

Perusing the enigmatic, bustling markets is a must-do on any trip to the city. Jaffa's flea market (see page 98), HaCarmel Market (see page 82) and Nachalat Binyamin Craft Market (see page 90) are all an entertaining and free way to spend a few hours.

None of Tel Aviv's museums now charges admission fees for children, making visiting them a low-cost family activity.

Students with an international student card also get up to
30 per cent off. What's more, the city's art galleries have free
entry for all.

The big green park in the north of the city is a great place to
have a picnic in the sunshine, rent inexpensive bicycles and cycle
along the paths, or use the basketball, volleyball and table-
tennis facilities for free.

🔺 The city's wide, sandy beaches are perfect for a cheap day out

When it rains

Thankfully, rainy days in Tel Aviv are few and far between and will only occur during the winter months. Should you be unlucky enough to visit on one of the days when the skies open, there are still plenty of activities to keep you entertained until the sun comes out again – and it won't be long before it does.

Rainy days are a great time to appreciate the city's varied and high-quality museums and art galleries. The world-class Tel Aviv Museum of Art (see page 71) and the sprawling exhibition halls of the Eretz Israel Museum (see page 68) are considered two of the best, but there are countless smaller museums, each interesting in its own right. From Ben Gurion House (see page 66), to Independence Hall where the declaration was signed (see page 86), to the Museum of the History of Tel Aviv & Jaffa (see page 70) and a clutch of independent art galleries, there is plenty of cultural appeal under covered roofs.

Watching a good film on the big screen is an excellent way to spend an evening, and the Tel Aviv Cinematheque (see page 71) shows a wide selection of arty flicks, some of which are in English. There are also mainstream cinemas in the Dizengoff Center, Dizengoff Square and the Azrieli Building, all of which show blockbusters and new releases in English with Hebrew subtitles. You could also join the throngs of Israelis in the Dizengoff Center or Azrieli Center for a spot of window-shopping and lunch.

Another great way to sit out the rain is to snuggle down in one of the city's many cafés with a good book and a steaming cup of coffee or herbal tea. All cafés offer free, fast Wi-Fi so this could be a good time to catch up on emails. Alternatively, have a leisurely meal in a restaurant – Israelis love to take their time over their food so don't feel you have to make a hasty exit once you've finished eating.

🔺 *Wandering the aisles of the Dizengoff Center*

On arrival

TIME DIFFERENCE
Tel Aviv, as with the rest of Israel, is two hours ahead of Greenwich Mean Time (GMT) and operates daylight saving, which occurs roughly between April and September.

ARRIVING
By air
Tel Aviv's Ben Gurion International Airport is the country's main port of entry and is located on Route 1, serving both Jerusalem and Tel Aviv. It is an efficient, modern airport with connections to airports around the world, and while security is predictably high, it is organised and relatively hassle-free. Be aware that on entering and leaving Israel you will be questioned. Comply, be open and friendly, and understand it is routine.

El Al (ⓦ www.elal.co.il) is Israel's national airline and competes favourably price-wise with other major airlines. The good news for Europeans is that there are now several budget airlines, such as **easyJet** (ⓦ www.easyjet.com), **Flybe** (ⓦ www.flybe.com) and **Air Berlin** (ⓦ www.airberlin.com), which offer low-cost flights.

Ben Gurion has good bus and train links with Tel Aviv and Jerusalem, and car-rental counters, open 24 hours a day, can be found in the arrivals terminal. The train is the best way into the city, taking 12 minutes to reach the centre and running every half hour, 24 hours a day. There are also buses, *sheruts* (minibus-style taxis) and regular taxis (see page 54).

By road

Tel Aviv's central location and position as Israel's business and economic hub mean that road networks in and around the area are plentiful. That said, dire congestion problems plague the city. Rush hour is particularly bad and best avoided.

Route 1 runs between Tel Aviv and Jerusalem, with two north-bound routes heading to cities such as Netanya and Haifa and off into Galilee. Route 4 is the older of the two, but the double-lane motorway of Route 2 will zip you up and down the Mediterranean coast much more quickly.

Parking in the city can also be a nightmare and it isn't uncommon for locals to have to drive around for over an hour looking for a parking spot after work. There are car parks but these can be extremely costly so it is worth checking with your hotel whether they offer free parking.

By train

Israel's railway network is still fairly new, but lines are growing each year and it now provides a good, affordable option for visitors to Tel Aviv. The city has four train stations, which, running from south to north, are: HaHaganah, HaShalom, Merkaz (known as Arlosorov) and Universita. Merkaz is considered the main railway station and is adjacent to the bus station of the same name. The main lines run along the Mediterranean coast and offer regular services to northern cities such as Haifa (taking 1 hour) and Akko (1 hour 40 minutes). A line runs to Jerusalem Malha Train Station (1 hour 30 minutes), but this takes longer than the bus and the train station is outside the city. A line also runs as far south as Beer Sheva.

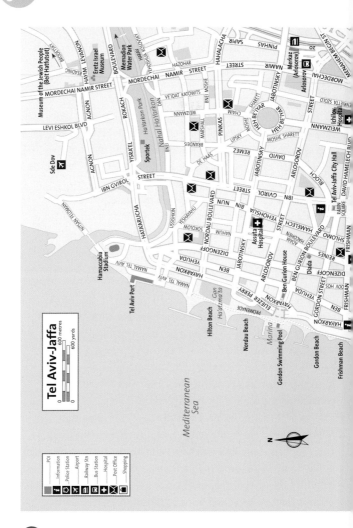

Tel Aviv-Jaffa

Mediterranean Sea

POI
Information
Police Station
Airport
Railway Stn
Bus Station
Hospital
Post Office
Shopping

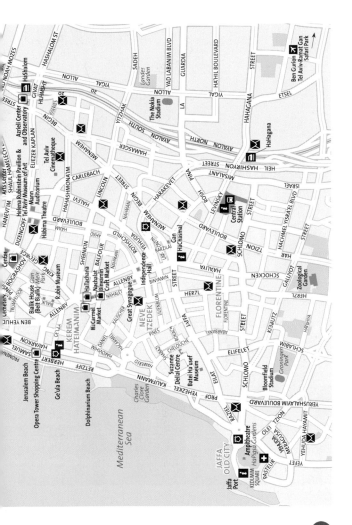

⬥ Jaffa's Old City lies to the south of Tel Aviv

By bus

Tel Aviv has two main bus stations: the central bus station
(ⓐ 106 Levinsky Rd) and Merkaz Bus Station (also known as
Arlosorov), which is adjacent to the main railway station. Inter-
city coaches are run by **Egged** (ⓦ www.egged.co.il) and form a
reliable and cost-effective way to get around the country. Most
depart from the central bus station but will also stop at Merkaz.
Bus 405 runs every 20 minutes to Jerusalem, taking one hour.

FINDING YOUR FEET

Tel Aviv is a busy, traffic-filled city, but it isn't a metropolis and
is easy to navigate. Despite news coverage of terrorism in Israel,
the chances of anything happening are very slim and security
is understandably and reassuringly high. Expect to be checked
with a metal detector and asked to open your handbag on
entering any public building. Crime within the city is relatively
low and while visitors should take common-sense precautions,
there is little to worry about. Theft is the most prevalent crime,
so keep an eye on your belongings and never leave anything
valuable in a car.

ORIENTATION

Tel Aviv is fringed by the Mediterranean to the west, HaYarkon
Park to the north, Jaffa to the south and the Ayalon Highway to
the east. While suburbs do expand beyond these perimeters,
the main part of the city sits snugly within them. The Dizengoff
Center is a useful central point, and Dizengoff Street a major
north–south artery. Ibn Gvirol Street is one of the main
thoroughfares into the city from the north, while Rothschild

Boulevard begins at the Habima Theatre complex and runs south. HaYarkon Street runs along the coast, with other major roads and boulevards running perpendicular to it. The Ayalon Highway – with the landmark features of the round, square and circular Azrieli buildings alongside it – takes traffic from and around the city to the airport and Jerusalem, north and south.

GETTING AROUND

Intra-city buses are run by **Dan** (Ⓦ www.dan.co.il) and are cheap and efficient, covering an extensive network. They charge a flat rate of 5.20NIS per journey. Head to the tourist information office on the promenade (see page 136) to pick up a map of city bus routes. Following the main bus routes are share taxis known as *sherut* which are minibuses that can be hailed anywhere along those routes (not just at designated bus stops). They cost marginally less than public buses and some run during Shabbat hours – the public ones don't.

Taxi drivers are required to run the meter although many try to get away with not doing so when picking up foreigners. Insist they start the meter or choose another taxi. Tip by rounding up to the nearest shekel; drivers sometimes ask for more, but this is not necessary. Taxis from Ben Gurion International Airport are strictly regulated. Do not accept a ride from anyone who stands inside the terminal – the 'legitimate' taxis are outside, clearly marked. The ride into Tel Aviv costs about 40NIS. Just to the north of Tel Aviv is Sde Dov Airport, which offers flights to Haifa (although this is only an hour by train) and Eilat. El Al, **Arkia** (Ⓦ www.arkia.com) and **Israir** (Ⓦ www.israirairlines.com) all offer flights from both Ben Gurion and Sde Dov. Sde Dov is

🔺 *Taxis are a reliable way of getting around the city*

served by easy and plentiful public transport, which includes city buses.

There are several bicycle-rental companies from which you can hire bikes for around 60NIS or scooters for 150NIS per day. Companies worth a try include **O-Fun** (ⓐ 197 Ben Yehuda St ⓣ 03 5442292 ⓦ www.rentabikeisrael.com) and **Cycle** (ⓐ 147 Ben Yehuda St ⓣ 03 5293037 ⓦ www.cycle.co.il).

Car hire

Car-rental companies tend to cluster along HaYarkon Street near the bottom of Frishman and Gordon streets, as well as in Ben Gurion Airport. Driving around the city is not recommended as parking is nightmarish and traffic congestion heavy. For getting out of Tel Aviv, however, a car will let you see much more of the country in a shorter space of time than by using public transport. Driving is on the left and you must be over 21 to rent a car. Some companies to try are:

Avis ⓐ 113 HaYarkon St ⓣ 03 5271752 and ⓐ Ben Gurion Airport ⓣ 03 9712315 ⓦ www.avis.co.il

Budget ⓐ 99 HaYarkon St ⓣ 03 9350012 and ⓐ Ben Gurion Airport ⓣ 03 9712315 ⓦ www.budget.co.il

Eldan ⓐ 114 HaYarkon St ⓣ 03 5271166 and ⓐ Ben Gurion Airport ⓣ 03 9773400 ⓦ www.eldan.co.il

Hertz ⓐ 144 HaYarkon St ⓣ 03 5223332 and ⓐ Ben Gurion Airport ⓣ 03 9772444 ⓦ www.hertz.co.il

● *Dizengoff Square is centrally located*

THE CITY OF
Tel Aviv

North-Central Tel Aviv

The city centre and north of Tel Aviv hold a surprisingly varied selection of attractions, from world-class museums to green parks and sprawling beaches, to art museums and historic cemeteries. This is the heart of the city, where business, leisure, retail therapy and fun collide. Cafés line the boulevards, restaurants compete with bars for prime locations, and huge areas of renovation have seen the emergence of cultural centres and leisure spots. No trip to Tel Aviv would be complete (or indeed possible) without visiting this lively, real and bubbly part of the city.

SIGHTS & ATTRACTIONS

Azrieli Observatory

The observatory, perched on top of the tallest of the three towering Azrieli buildings, proffers incredible bird's-eye views over the whole of Tel Aviv. Gaze across the low-rise rooftops to the glittering blue sea, as far north as HaYarkon Park and down to Jaffa's Old City. ❸ 49th floor, round building ❶ 03 6081179 ❶ 09.30–18.00 daily (winter); 09.30–20.00 Sat–Thur, 09.30–18.00 Fri (summer) ❶ Admission charge

Beaches: Hilton, Nordau, Gordon & Frishman

Tel Aviv's beaches are one of its undoubted highlights. Wide stretches of golden sand lead down to the warm Mediterranean Sea where Tel Avivis come to cool off in the height of summer. The beaches are well equipped with lifeguards, shade, sunbeds,

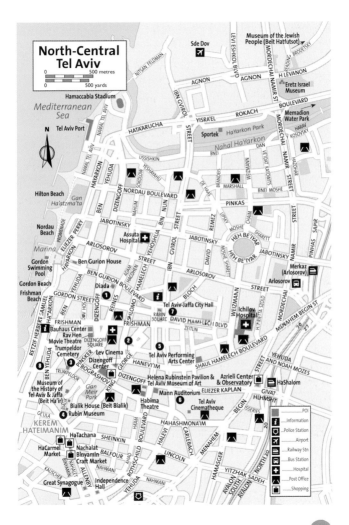

North-Central Tel Aviv

0 — 500 metres
0 — 500 yards

Mediterranean Sea

Hamaccabia Stadium

Sde Dov ✈

Museum of the Jewish People (Beit Hatfutsot)

Eretz Israel Museum

AGNON

LEVI ESHKOL BLVD

AGNON

MORDECHAI NAMIR ST

FEDING ROAD

BRODETSKY

H. LEVANON

HARAV KOSOVSKY

BOULEVARD

Memadion Water Park

Tel Aviv Port

HATA'ARUCHA

YISRA'EL

ROKACH

Sportek

HaYarkon Park

Nahal HaYarkon

DAN

BNEI

MORDECHAI NAMIR ST

HADAR

USSISHKIN

YESHARAHU

DE HAAS

BRANDES

MARSHALL

BNEI MOSHE

NIZHUM

VEDAT KATOVITS

NAMIR STREET

SAPIR

Hilton Beach

Gan Ha'atzma'ta

NORDAU BOULEVARD

BIN NUN

PINKAS

JABOTINSKY

LIPSKY

CHAIM

Nordau Beach

Promenade

ARLOSOROV

YEHOSHUA

IBN GVIROL

JABOTINSKY

MOSHE

HEH BE'IYAR

HEH BE'IYAR

JABOTINSKY

NAMIR

PINHAS

Assuta Hospital ✚

Marina

ADAM HACOHEN

DAVID

MOSHE SHARETT

ARLOSOROV

Gordon Swimming Pool

Ben Gurion House

BEN GURION BOULEVARD

HAMELECH

BLOCH

Merkaz (Arlosorov) 🚉

Arlosorov 🚌

Gordon Beach

Frishman Beach

RETZIF HERBERT SAMUEL

HA'YARKON

BEN YEHUDA

GORDON STREET

Diada ❶

SHLOMO

REINES

Tel Aviv-Jaffa City Hall ❼

WEIZMANN

MENACHEM BEGIN ST

YEHUDA AND NOAH MOZES

FRISHMAN

DIZENGOFF

RABIN SQUARE

DAVID HAMELECH BLVD

Ichilov Hospital ✚

HaShalom 🚉

Bauhaus Center ℹ Rav Hen Movie Theatre

DIZENGOFF SQUARE

ZEITLIN

Trumpeldor Cemetery

Lev Cinema Dizengoff Center ❷

HANEVI'M

SHAUL HAMELECH BOULEVARD

Azrieli Center & Observatory

GIVAT

PINKER

BOGRASHOV

KING GEORGE

❺

Tel Aviv Performing Arts Center

ELIEZER KAPLAN

BEGIN

HLIHMSH'T

❽

TRUMPELDOR

DIZENGOFF

Helena Rubinstein Pavilion & Tel Aviv Museum of Art

ISSERIES

Museum of the History of Tel Aviv & Jaffa (Beit Ha'ir)

Gan Meir Park

HAM

Mann Auditorium

Tel Aviv Cinematheque ❻

Bialik House (Beit Bialik)

Habima Theatre

HAHASHMONA'IM

GE'ULA

Rubin Museum ❹

KEREM HATEIMANIM

HaTachana

SHEINKIN

ROTHSCHILD BOULEVARD

HALEV

CARLEBACH

MENAHEM

HAMASGER

HaCarmel Market

Nachalat Binyamin Craft Market

BALFOUR

LINCOLN

NORTH

AYALON

NAHMANI

AHAD

NAHMANI

YITZHAK SADEH

Great Synagogue

Independence Hall

ALLENBY

YEHUDA

AYALON SOUTH

KAUSCHR

BINYAMIN

NAHLAT

Legend

■ POI
ℹ Information
👮 Police Station
✈ Airport
🚉 Railway Stn
🚌 Bus Station
✚ Hospital
✉ Post Office
🛍 Shopping

and toilet and shower blocks, as well as cafés and restaurants with tables dug into the sand. There are also the compulsory exercise bars so toned army recruits can show off their muscles to the pedestrians ambling along the promenade.

Each beach has its own vibe, and together they reflect the eclectic and varied demographics of this cosmopolitan city. **Hilton Beach** is so named for the towering Hilton Hotel which looms over it. It is in fact a rather unusual beach in that it attracts three very distinct groups of sun-seekers. One end is known as the gay beach and has a lively, fun atmosphere, while the other end is the dog beach and is the only stretch of Tel Aviv's beaches where pups can race across the sand – not much fun for those wanting to sunbathe. Thanks to a breakwater, the Hilton Beach also has good surf and young surfers come to ride the waves.

Next along, heading south, is **Nordau Beach**, the city's religious beach. Single-sex beach days allow those abiding by religious law time to enjoy the summer sun and waves. Women's days are on Sunday, Tuesday and Thursday while men's days are Monday, Wednesday and Friday.

Right in the middle of the city are **Gordon Beach** and **Frishman Beach**, which cater to the average Israeli. These busy, pretty beaches boast the widest expanses of sand, a good range of amenities and an anything-goes atmosphere. The promenade here is always busy and is infused with a true seaside atmosphere (see page 78 for more beaches).

Gan Meir Park

Located just behind the Dizengoff Center on the east side of King George Street is Gan Meir Park, a small but popular

⬥ *The modern skyscrapers of the Azrieli Center*

area of parkland. Green lawns, a children's playground, an enclosed dog park and an ornamental pond make it a pleasant respite from the hubbub of the city centre. On summer evenings musicians appear to entertain relaxing Tel Avivis and it is a pleasant place in which to sit and enjoy a falafel lunch. The park was opened in 1944 before Israel's declaration of independence and later named after Meir Dizengoff, the city's first mayor.

HaYarkon Park
Spanning the city's northern entrance, HaYarkon Park provides the green respite so needed in Tel Aviv. Come summer Israeli families, couples and youngsters appear to laze under the shade of trees, have barbecues and picnics or use the free basketball, volleyball and table-tennis facilities. A small boating lake, cycle paths and the Sportek adventure sports complex, provide plenty for energetic types to do. And for those simply wanting to relax in a pleasant, green environment, the park is an ideal escape from the sweltering summer heat of the city.

Rabin Square
Rabin Square isn't really much to look at on first glance. The 1980s-style municipal building that stands at its foot is rather unappealing, and traffic whizzes around the square which fringes busy Ibn Gvirol Street. Yet the square is a Tel Aviv landmark for it is here that crowds gather to celebrate festivals, holidays and Independence Day, to voice their opinions at political rallies, to sing along to concerts or simply to walk their dog and play Frisbee.

The square was originally named Kings of Israel Square but following the shock assassination of Prime Minister Yitzhak Rabin in 1995 when he was speaking at a peace rally, it was renamed in his honour. A memorial has been erected just under the municipal building to mark the spot where he was killed.

Tel Aviv Port
Where the Yarkon River reaches the Mediterranean Sea is Tel Aviv's old port. It has been many years since ships chugged in and out of the port, and it quickly declined into a run-down,

◆ *Enjoying the sunny weather in HaYarkon Park*

🔺 *Rabin Square is a busy local meeting point*

disused area. A major overhaul, however, has since seen trendy restaurants and cafés emerge alongside pumping bars and nightclubs that attract scores of partying youngsters and big-name bands and DJs. A wooden promenade provides a pleasant seaside walk after a big Israeli brunch – if you ignore the view of the power plant in the distance! Today it is a big part of the city's entertainment scene and a pleasant respite from the centre on hot, humid summer days.

Trumpeldor Cemetery

Hidden away in the city centre and easy to miss is the old Jewish Trumpeldor Cemetery, created in 1902 just before the city was founded. Here many of the famous and influential figures of Tel Aviv's past have been laid to rest and it is an interesting place to spend an hour. Among the famous graves of Zionists, politicians, authors and artists can be found those of Chaim Nahman Bialik, one of Israel's most famous poets, Meir Dizengoff, the first mayor of Tel Aviv, and Nachum Gutman, the Israeli artist. For those who can read Hebrew many of the tombs have biographies of the interred, and for those who can't there's the option of a guided tour run by the **Association for Tourism** (☏ 03 5166188 ❶ Admission charge). ⓐ 19 Trumpeldor St

CULTURE

Bauhaus Center

Tel Aviv's large number of Bauhaus-style buildings have awarded it both UNESCO World Heritage status and the nickname 'The White City' (see page 88). The style is understated and easy to miss but a visit to the Bauhaus Center can shed some light on this simplistic German architectural style that has come to define the city. The small shop located on Dizengoff Street sells books, art, postcards and souvenirs as well as exhibits, guided tours or audio guides. ⓐ 99 Dizengoff St ⓘ 03 5220249 ⓛ 10.00–19.30 Sun–Thur, 10.00–14.30 Fri, 12.00–19.30 Sat

Ben Gurion House

Although Israel's first prime minister far preferred the isolated solitude of the Negev Desert, he spent many years living in Tel Aviv both before and after the founding of the State of Israel (see box). He bequeathed his house to the people of the city and today it remains as it did when he lived there. Within the museum-memorial are exhibits of Ben Gurion's interesting and influential life, including photographs, documents and personal items. ⓐ 17 Ben Gurion St ⓘ 03 5221010 ⓛ 08.00–17.00 Mon, 08.00–15.00 Tues–Thur & Sun, 08.00–13.00 Fri

Bialik House (Beit Bialik)

Chaim Bialik is Israel's most famous and acclaimed poet. Ukranian-born Bialik moved to Palestine in 1924 following great success in Europe, and set about building his dream house on the street named in his honour. The building itself is attractive and is adorned inside with Jewish decorative motifs. While most of the information inside the house is in Hebrew, the rooms and building are in themselves interesting for a glimpse into old Tel Aviv architecture and style. ⓐ 22 Bialik St ⓘ 03 6042222

DAVID BEN GURION

Israel's first prime minister was the hugely influential Zionist David Ben Gurion (1886–1973), who has been voted as one of TIME™ Magazine's 100 most influential people of the 20th century. Ben Gurion was born in Poland to Zionist parents and, at the age of 20, he arrived in the Holy Land and became hugely active in political circles. Throughout the late Ottoman period and during the British Mandate period, Ben Gurion was a member of the Socialist-Zionist group and then the Jewish Legion. He was a founder of trade unions and a representative in the World Zionist Organisation and Jewish Agency. It was also at this time that he met and married his wife Paula.

Ben Gurion signed the declaration of independence on 14 May 1948, and shortly after became the new country's first elected prime minister. Having been a massive force in achieving this Jewish dream, it seemed apt that he would then be elected to lead the country through its first few tumultuous years. Throughout his almost 20 years as prime minister he led the country to victory in the 1948 Arab-Israeli War and the 1956 Sinai War, encouraged vast Jewish immigration from around the world, oversaw the airlifting of hundreds of Jews out of Arab countries, instigated the building of countless towns and villages, and developed infrastructure.

Ben Gurion and his wife are today buried in his retirement kibbutz of Sde Boker in the Negev Desert, a region he loved passionately.

🕐 11.00–17.00 Mon–Thur, 10.00–14.00 Fri & Sat
ⓘ Admission charge

Eretz Israel Museum

A series of pavilions spreading across the north of HaYarkon Park house one of the country's biggest museums. The Eretz Israel Museum is dedicated to the history and culture of this complex land from the ancient invaders who conquered it to the declaration of independence less than a century ago. A wealth of state-of-the-art multimedia displays and a planetarium both add appeal. Temporary and permanent exhibits range from glassware to coins and pottery as well as ethnographic items and Judaica. Of particular interest are the Nechushtan Pavilion, which displays a reconstruction of a Bronze Age mine, and a full reproduction of an ancient olive press. ⓐ 2 Hayim Levanon St ⓣ 03 6415244 ⓦ www.eretz museum.org.il 🕐 10.00–16.00 Sun–Wed, 10.00–20.00 Thur, 10.00–14.00 Fri & Sat ⓘ Admission charge

Habima Theatre

Israel's national theatre was originally founded in Moscow in 1918 and moved to Tel Aviv in 1931. The troupe of 80 actors puts on several plays a day, most of which are in Hebrew (although simultaneous translation is available). In a country where theatre and the arts are flourishing, the Habima Theatre is considered the pinnacle. Tickets, which regularly sell out, can be bought from box offices along Ibn Gvirol and Dizengoff streets or from the theatre itself. ⓐ Habima Sq, Tarshat Av ⓣ 03 6295555 ⓦ www.habima.co.il

Helena Rubenstein Pavilion

This art gallery began life in 1959 to act as an extension of the Tel Aviv Museum of Art (see page 71); its reputation has soared and today it is highly respected in its own right. Located alongside the main museum, it houses works by both established and emerging Israeli artists. The exhibits, some of which are free, and others accessed with a ticket for the main museum, change regularly and are wide-ranging in their styles and themes. ⓐ 6 Tarsat Blvd ⓣ 03 5287196 ⓛ 10.00–16.00 Mon, Wed & Sat, 10.00–22.00 Tues & Thur

◭ *Discover ancient artefacts at the Eretz Israel Museum*

Mann Auditorium

The highly acclaimed Tel Aviv Philharmonic Orchestra plays sell-out performances at the Mann Auditorium in the city centre. Tickets can be purchased from the box offices on Ibn Gvirol and Dizengoff streets or from the auditorium itself, but they can be hard to come by – the auditorium boasts one of the highest numbers of season-ticket holders in the world. ⓐ 1 Huberman St ⓣ 03 6211777 ⓦ www.hatarbut.co.il

Museum of the History of Tel Aviv & Jaffa (Beit Ha'ir)

Situated in the impressive, newly renovated town hall opposite Bialik Square, this museum and cultural complex is known locally as Beit Ha'ir (which translates as 'town hall'). Exhibits range from different aspects of the city to a profile on Meir Dizengoff, to a virtual display room with an interactive timeline. Beit Ha'ir is part of a cultural complex that includes Bialik Square and several museums located along the square which together were awarded UNESCO World Heritage status. ⓐ 27 Bialik St ⓣ 03 5253403 ⓒ 09.00–17.00 Mon–Thur, 10.00–14.00 Fri & Sat ⓘ Admission charge

Museum of the Jewish People (Beit Hatfutsot)

Located within the grounds of Tel Aviv University is this museum, also known as Beit Hatfutsot – the first and largest museum of Jewish history in the world. Multimedia displays and presentations follow the trials of the Jewish people over the centuries, exploring their culture, religion, ethnography and history. In addition, temporary exhibits add a further layer of interest, bringing to life themes such as music, weddings and art and providing profiles of influential Jews from around the world. ⓐ Tel Aviv University ⓣ 03 6408000 ⓦ www.bh.org.il ⓛ 10.00–16.00 Sun–Tues, 10.00–20.00 Wed & Thur, 09.00–13.00 Fri ⓘ Admission charge

Rubin Museum

Part of the cultural complex of buildings along Bialik Square, this museum/art gallery showcases the works of acclaimed Israeli artist Reuven Rubin (1893–1974). The building it occupies was once the artist's house, which he bequeathed to the city. Displays and exhibits on his life are shown alongside some his most famous paintings. ⓐ 14 Bialik St ⓣ 03 5255961 ⓦ www.rubinmuseum.org.il ⓛ 10.00–15.00 Mon & Wed–Fri, 10.00–20.00 Tues, 11.00–14.00 Sat ⓘ Admission charge

Tel Aviv Cinematheque

Israeli cinema is growing in popularity, with several successful films emerging from the country in recent years. The cinematheque, together with the Spielberg Film Archives in Jerusalem, forms Israel's cinematic core and shows a wide-ranging selection of art films, whose hard-hitting and sensitive themes invariably invite either harsh criticism or fierce acclaim. There is a yearly film festival held in November. ⓐ Ha'arba'a St ⓣ 03 6060800 ⓘ Admission charge

Tel Aviv Museum of Art

Tel Aviv's Museum of Art is one of the world's finest art galleries, and one of Israel's leading cultural attractions. It started out in 1932 in what was later to become Independence Hall (see

⬥ The Tel Aviv Museum of Art is a big attraction

page 86), and moved to its current location in 1971, a large and unremarkable building in the heart of the city.

The outside may not be much to look at but the displays are hugely impressive, even to art novices. Different wings display collections of classical and contemporary works by Israeli and international artists – including the likes of Picasso, Miró, Monet, Renoir, Cezanne, Matisse and Chagall. The temporary exhibits, photography wing and sculpture garden are also worth visiting. Adjacent to the main museum is the Helena Rubenstein Pavilion (see page 69). ⓐ 27 Shaul Hamelech Blvd ⓣ 03 6077020 ⓦ www.tamuseum.com ⓛ 10.00–16.00 Mon, Wed & Sat, 10.00–22.00 Tues & Thur ⓘ Admission charge

RETAIL THERAPY

Shopping opportunities in Tel Aviv tend to cluster around several areas, each with their own speciality. The north-central region is characterised by long shopping streets and centres, including the Dizengoff Center (ⓐ Corner of Dizengoff and King George streets ⓣ 03 6212416 ⓛ 09.00–24.00 Sun–Thur, 09.00–16.00 Fri, 20.00–24.00 Sat) – the country's first and best-loved mall. Despite its 1980s appearance, rather jumbled maze of walkways and strange selection of shops, it is always busy and a hub of Tel Aviv life. Cafés, small eateries, a cinema, supermarket and high-street shops such as Castro and Fox can be found alongside toy and sportswear shops, shoes, jewellery, home appliances and even a whole shop dedicated to jigsaws. On Friday mornings, the Dizengoff food fair sees the aisles and walkways packed with stalls that sell a wide variety of taster dishes.

Dizengoff Street is also a major shopping area, and heading north from the shopping centre are a mixture of gaudy wedding-dress shops, clothes shops, cheap and expensive shoe shops, bookshops, cafés and juice bars.

On the eastern side of the city is the Azrieli Center (🅐 123 Menachem Begin St 🕿 03 6081179 🔘 www.azrieli center.co.il 🕓 10.00–22.00 Sun–Thur, 09.30–17.00 Fri, 20.00–23.00 Sat), which is home to the country's biggest shopping centre. It is impossible to miss the Azrieli Center skyscrapers that have become a feature of the Tel Aviv skyline. The round, square and triangular buildings are home to one of the Middle East's biggest business centres, and even an observatory (see page 58) as well as the shopping centre. More upmarket than the Dizengoff Center, it is home to higher-priced clothes shops and designer boutiques.

TAKING A BREAK

Tel Aviv enjoys no end of excellent places to grab a coffee or a bite to eat. For traditional falafel or newly fashionable *sabich* make for the corner of Dizengoff and Frishman streets, where you'll find a cluster of small stalls, open all day. If it's sandwiches you're after, jostle with the young and trendy for a spot at one of the bars dotted along Ben Gurion Boulevard. These are always busy, and serve sushi, breakfasts and good-quality coffee as well as fresh, made-to-order doorstop sandwiches.

Café Jo £ ❶ Long-standing, popular café in a prime location on the corner of Dizengoff and Gordon streets. Grab a copy of

Haaretz English-language newspaper, bag a pavement and enjoy a perfectly brewed coffee in the middle of the enigmatic hubbub of the city centre. @ 130 Dizengoff St ❶ 03 5272533 🕒 24 hrs daily

Falafel HaKosem (The Wizard) £ ❷ The charismatic owner dishes out freshly cooked falafel, *shawarma* and *sabich* to the queues of hungry customers at this simple falafel bar. @ 174 HaNevi'im St ❶ 03 5252033 🕒 10.00–23.00 Sun–Thur

Mashwesha £ ❸ Don't miss this rustic eatery serving up some of the city's best hummus. The place is tiny, but there are small tables outside and the food is fantastic. @ 40 Pinsker St ❶ 03 6293796 🕒 11.00–23.00 Sun–Thur, 11.00–17.00 Fri, 12.00–23.00 Sat

Café Bialik ££ ❹ This café is a welcome pit stop from all the museums along the cultural hub that is newly renovated Bialik Street. It has a full menu ranging from breakfasts and sandwiches to main meals and often hosts live music. @ 2 Bialik St ❶ 03 6200832 🕒 08.00–late Sun–Fri, 11.00–late Sat

AFTER DARK

RESTAURANTS

Giraffe Noodle Bar ££ ❺ The incredible popularity of this noodle bar means it is now a small chain with branches across the country. Asian fare ranging from noodles to sushi to dumplings to rice dishes (and some sumptuous desserts) is cheap, tasty and filling. More than just a fast-food joint, Giraffe oozes laid-back sociable cool. ⓐ 49 Ibn Gvirol St ⓣ 03 6916294 ⓛ 12.00–01.00 daily

Goocha ££ ❻ When the queues at the original place simply got too long, the owners of Goocha opened a second branch of this incredibly popular and refreshingly affordable seafood restaurant along Ibn Gvirol. The décor is bright and modern with outdoor tables and bar seats, and the food is fresh and creatively cooked. The calamari is a big favourite. ⓐ 171 Dizengoff St ⓣ 03 5222886 and ⓐ 14 Ibn Gvirol St ⓣ 03 6911603 ⓛ 12.00–02.00 daily

Brasserie £££ ❼ This is one of the city's best-loved restaurants and seems to reflect the vibe of those who live here. Trendy yet unpretentiously chic it has three distinct menus for the different times of the day (breakfast, lunch and dinner), a cuisine of elegant French/Mediterranean bistro dishes and views of Rabin Square. ⓐ 70 Ibn Gvirol St ⓣ 03 6967111 ⓛ 24 hrs daily

Rafael £££ ❽ Run by one of the country's top chefs, Rafael is often voted the best restaurant in the whole of Tel Aviv. Traditional French and Mediterranean food is jazzed up with Moroccan and Middle Eastern spices and cooking styles with impressive and tasty results. Be sure to ask for a table with a sea view. A lunch menu is offered from 12.00–15.00 Sun–Thur. ⓐ Adiv Hotel, 87 HaYarkon St ⓣ 03 5226464 ⓛ 12.00–15.00, 19.00–late daily

BARS & CLUBS

Erlich The latest tunes pump loudly across this trendy, popular haunt, where scantily clad partygoers dance and drink the night away. ⓐ Tel Aviv Port ⓣ 03 5466728 ⓛ 21.30–late daily

Friends One of the city's few long-standing bars, Friends has managed to remain a firm feature on Tel Aviv's nightlife scene for years now. It is dark, loud and crowded and resembles more of a nightclub than a bar – which is exactly how its (mostly single) patrons like it. ⓐ 186 Ben Yehuda St ⓣ 054 8035757 ⓛ 20.00–late daily

Helen and Morti Bar A chilled-out vibe, welcoming locals, lively music and a well-stocked bar make this place a great alternative to the loud pick-up bars around. ⓐ 196 Ben Yehuda Sl ⓣ 077 2177766 ⓛ 19.00–late daily

The Fifth Dimension This big hangar in the port is the perfect arena for top Israeli and international bands to pump out their latest sounds to throngs of revellers. **Hangar 11** nearby also hosts big-name acts such as The Prodigy when they come to the city. ⓐ Tel Aviv Port ⓣ 03 6024559 ⓛ 22.00–late daily ⓘ Admission charge

South Tel Aviv

South Tel Aviv is characterised by varied neighbourhoods connected by long streets. There is an undeniable atmosphere of artistic, bohemian flair, with the residents' creativity evident in the number of small art galleries, craft markets, designer boutiques and organic cafés that can be found here. Yet tradition still holds a place, as the age-old HaCarmel Market, the religious neighbourhood of Kerem HaTeimanim (Yemenite Vineyard) and the Great Synagogue all attest. What the area lacks in big museums and attractions, it makes up for in charming – if not beautiful – quarters, fashionable yet unpretentious shopping streets and delightful stretches of beach.

SIGHTS & ATTRACTIONS

Beaches: Jerusalem, Ge'ula & Dolphinarium

The string of beaches that start in the north of the city and spread their way along the coastline are one of Tel Aviv's most aesthetically pleasing features. Following on south from the beaches of the north and the city centre (see page 58), is **Jerusalem Beach** – an enjoyable place to spend an afternoon, crammed with small cafés, colourful Italian ice-cream parlours and the stylish Opera Tower Shopping Centre. Just south of here is **Ge'ula Beach**, known more commonly as Banana Beach after the Banana Café located there. It attracts those looking for a quieter, more relaxed beach, where you can unwind with a good book, play *matkot* (bat and ball) or cool off with a drink in the

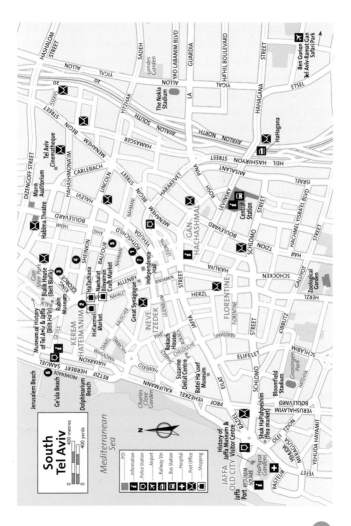

South Tel Aviv

0 metres 400
0 yards 400

POI
- Information
- Police Station
- Airport
- Railway Stn
- Bus Station
- Hospital
- Post Office
- Shopping

Mediterranean Sea

N

STREET HASHALOM
AYALON 20
AYALON 20
SADEH
Landes Garden
YAD LABANIM BLVD
GUARDIA
STREET
Ben Gurion
Tel Aviv-Ramat Gan Safari Park

ISSERLIS
STREET BEGIN
YITZHAK
AYALON SOUTH
The Nokia Stadium
LA
AYALON NORTH
YIGAL
HA'FHIL BOULEVARD
HAHAGANA
ETSEL

DIZENGOFF STREET
STREET BEGIN
MENAHEM
HAMASGER
HaHagana

Tel Aviv Cinematheque
HAHASHMONAIM
CARLEBACH
HARAKEVET
PIN
HASHIRON STREET
MISALANT
HEIL
ISRAEL

Mann Auditorium
HALEVI
LINCON
STREET
MENAHEM BEGIN STREET
ROSH
LEVINSKY
Central Station
STREET
HACHMEI YISRAEL BLVD

Habima Theatre
BOULEVARD
HA'AM
NAHMANI
YEHUDA
GAN HACHASHMAL
SCHLOMO
TZION
STREET
HAR

Gan Meir Park
SHEINKIN
ROTHSCHILD
BALFOUR
Independence Hall
BINYAMIN
HALIVA
SCHOCKEN
Zoological Garden
GALUYOT
HERZL

Bialik House (Beit Bialik)
KING GEORGE
HaTachana
Nachalat Binyamin Craft Market
ALLENBY
Great Synagogue
STREET
HERZL
FLORENTINE
STREET
KIBBUTZ

Museum of History of Tel Aviv & Jaffa
Rubin Museum
KEREM HATEIMANIM
HaCarmel Market
NEVE ZEDEK
NAHALE
JAFFA
FLORENTINE
ABARBANEL
SCHLIABIM

Jerusalem Beach
HERBERT SAMUEL
PROMENADE
RETZIF
HAYARKON
DANIEL
AHAD
Rokach House
Suzanne Dellal Centre
Batei Ha'osef Museum
ELIFELET
Groningen Park
HATIKVA

Ge'ula Beach
Dolphinarium Beach
Charles Clore Garden
YAMEED
SHALUSH
CHELOUCHE
PROF YEHEZKEL KAUFMANN
EILAT
SCHLOMO
Bloomfield Stadium
YERUSHALAYIM BOULEVARD

History of Jaffa Museum & Jaffa OLD CITY Visitor Centre
RAZIEL
Shuk HaPishpeshim (flea market)
NOTZL
ABULAFIA
YEHUDA HAYAMIT

JAFFA
Jaffa Port
KEDUMIM SQUARE
HaPisga Gardens
PASTEUR
YEFET

79

café. Films are also screened here for free in the evenings. Last along this stretch is funky **Dolphinarium Beach**, which caters to the young, hippy set who spend the days surfing and the balmy summer evenings banging away on bongo drums, strumming their guitars and making campfires. The **Surfpoint** (🕿 159 9567888) watersports centre offers courses and equipment rental for windsurfing, kite-surfing, scuba diving and kayaking.

Florentine neighbourhood

At first glance it is difficult to see what the fuss is about this southern neighbourhood. The tangle of somewhat dilapidated buildings is home to some of the city's poorest residents, and the area is generally rundown. Yet there is something undeniably charming about it. Bohemian cafés, offbeat artists' shops and restaurants and bars have set up here, their young owners attracted by cheap rent and the unconventionality of the area.

Great Synagogue

Tel Aviv has some 350 synagogues, although modest structures and décor mean they are all too easy to miss. The Great Synagogue is certainly not. Located on the southern end of Allenby Street, it is an imposing solid square building with a rounded dome and stained-glass windows. It was built in 1926, but extensive renovations in the 1970s succeeded in giving it a kind of ornate beauty rarely seen in other synagogues. Shabbat services are open to everyone, but modest and appropriate dress must be worn. 🅐 110 Allenby St 🕿 03 5604905

○ Tel Aviv's coast is lined with attractive beaches

HaCarmel Market

HaCarmel Market is one of the best-loved and most character-filled places in Tel Aviv – a lively, traditional Middle Eastern institution in a city of shopping centres and boutiques. The market is a long, tunnel-like lane of rudimentary stalls, shouting vendors and exotic aromas. Frying pans, T-shirts and scarves dangle above your head, fresh fruit and vegetables can be bought at a fraction of supermarket prices, colourful spices, nuts and sweet desserts are tantalising and delicious, and small hummus joints and cafés can be found tucked in behind the main market street.

HaTachana

This is the newest addition to Tel Aviv's leisure scene, and is proving hugely popular with the city's residents. HaTachana – which translates as 'train station' – is an impressive Ottoman-era construction that once linked Jaffa to Jerusalem via rail. A long and costly renovation project has seen the dilapidated area restored to its former glory and now a large cultural centre is home to cafés, galleries and boutiques, and hosts summer concerts and exhibitions. ● 03 609995 ● 10.00–22.00 Sat–Thur, 10.00–17.00 Fri

Kerem HaTeimanim (Yemenite Vineyard) neighbourhood

In a busy, noisy, secular city, the Yemenite Vineyard neighbourhood provides a well needed respite. It was founded in 1902 by Yemenite Jews and has long been known as one of the most religiously observant areas of the city, tucked away behind the busy HaCarmel Market. For years it was a rather

● *The bustling HaCarmel Market*

● *Neve Tzedek is Tel Aviv's oldest neighbourhood*

run-down area, with crumbling buildings and narrow, unkempt streets. Recently, however, the neighbourhood has become one of the most fashionable parts of the city, and property prices have soared. Traditional Yemenite restaurants are tucked away in side streets, bougainvillea plants wind their way up the fronts of balconied buildings and an air of religious adherence permeates throughout.

Neve Tzedek neighbourhood

When 60 Jewish Zionist families moved out of Jaffa in 1910 to found the new neighbourhood of Neve Tzedek they could never have imagined the thriving, cosmopolitan city that would emerge from it. In more recent years it suffered a phase of decline: the buildings became dilapidated and the area run-down. In the 1980s, however, the city municipality embarked on a massive project to renovate the area and honour it as the founding neighbourhood of modern Tel Aviv. Today it is one of the city's trendiest areas and emanates a relaxed, creative atmosphere where art galleries prosper and swish cafés are constantly crowded. When window-shopping in the designer boutiques, handmade jewellery shops and craft outlets, be sure to look out for **Rokach House** (❷ 36 Shimon Rokach St), one of Neve Tzedek's first buildings and therefore one of Tel Aviv's oldest.

Rothschild Boulevard

If asked to pick a place that epitomises Tel Aviv, most locals would surely plump for Rothschild Boulevard. The wide tree-lined street starts at the Habima Theatre in the north, finishes at Neve Tzedek in the south and has a large central walkway where much of the city's action takes place. With the exception of its Bauhaus architecture and Independence Hall (see below), there isn't an awful lot to see, but formal sights aren't what draw the weekend crowds. Strolling, cycling, roller-skating and dog-walking locals weave around the small children's play parks, and sandwich bars, cafés and restaurants line the pavements. At the weekend, impromptu recitals are held as people lounge on the grass to listen to musicians strumming away at their guitars – people-watching paradise. To get a true feel for the essence of Tel Aviv come on Friday morning when it is shoulder-to-shoulder in the cafés, big brunches are served up and anticipation of the weekend hangs in the air.

Sheinkin Street

This has long been considered one of the city's trendiest hotspots, and while some predict overshadowing by other up-and-coming neighbourhoods, something about this street says it will remain one of *the* places to be. Small clothes boutiques, shoe shops galore, colourful fruit-juice bars, tattoo parlours and several of Tel Aviv's best-loved cafés vie for attention, and there is a distinct atmosphere of boho-glamour.

CULTURE

Independence Hall

Number 16 Rothschild Boulevard has had a colourful and interesting past. It started out as Meir Dizengoff's house, and in 1930 the city's first mayor bequeathed it to the city, at which time it became the first home of the Tel Aviv Museum of Art

Sheinkin Street is lined with trendy boutiques

(see page 71). Most significantly, it was in this building that Israel's declaration of independence was signed on 14 May 1948. The event was presided over by David Ben Gurion, a top political figure and later Israel's first prime minister, and everything in the room looks as it did on that day. Cameras, flags, broadcasting equipment, paintings and furniture (some original, some reconstructed) have been placed with precision. The museum makes an interesting stop when walking along Rothschild Boulevard, and an hour is plenty of time to have a look around. **ⓐ** 16 Rothschild Blvd **ⓣ** 03 5173942 **ⓛ** 09.00–14.00 Sun–Fri **ⓘ** Admission charge

BAUHAUS ARCHITECTURE

Few would argue that Tel Aviv is a beautiful city. Yet thanks to its abundance of buildings constructed in the Bauhaus architectural style, it was, in 2003, awarded UNESCO World Heritage status. Bauhaus is not an ornate or classically beautiful style, yet its clean, simple lines are pleasing to the eye – unadorned and functional, with rounded balconies and white walls. Many of the city's 4,000-plus Bauhaus buildings were constructed in the 1930s by architects emigrating from Germany, and have earnt Tel Aviv the nickname 'the White City'. The concentration of Bauhaus architecture along Rothschild Boulevard makes it one of the best places to appreciate the style. Check out the following building numbers: 61, 66, 67, 73, 83, 84, 87, 89–91, 93, 99, 100, 117, 118, 119, 121, 123 and 126–8.

◔ *The Bauhaus style of architecture*

Nachalat Binyamin Craft Market

Twice a week the city's artists convene to display their talents at this lovely outdoor fair. Adjacent to the northern entrance of HaCarmel Market, it is a fun, colourful and interesting place to spend a couple of hours. Reasonably priced items can be bought while artists ply their craft to the entertainment of the crowds. Clowns, fortune-tellers and street performers add to the entertaining and light-hearted market experience.

RETAIL THERAPY

The south of Tel Aviv undoubtedly has the most interesting, varied shopping in the city. Offbeat, fashionable boutiques can be found alongside traditional markets and craft shops, which cluster in newly renovated neighbourhoods or along trendy streets, where café culture and shopping go hand in hand. Sheinkin Street (see page 86), HaCarmel Market (see page 82) and Nachalat Binyamin Craft Market (see above) are all worth visiting, even if you have no intention of buying anything. Another hotspot is the Electric Garden neighbourhood Gan HaChashmal – one of Tel Aviv's coolest and a relatively new addition to the scene. Shops vary from one-of-a-kind clothes boutiques to stores selling handcrafted jewellery, handbags and accessories.

The district was once the city's electrical plant and later suffered a few dark years of dilapidation until a group of fashion designers decided quite literally to set up shop here. It encompasses the area between the streets of Allenby, Yehuda Halevi, Barzilay and HaHashmal.

TAKING A BREAK

Café Hillel £ ❶ Part of a very successful chain, this café has a nice outside deck which, if you are lucky enough to get a seat, is the best place for soaking up the atmosphere of charismatic Rothschild Boulevard. It has excellent coffees as well as sandwiches, quiches, wraps and cakes. ⓐ 65 Rothschild Blvd ☎ 03 5288666 🕐 07.00–01.00 Sun–Thur, 07.00–Shabbat Fri, end of Shabbat–01.00 Sat

Humus Shlomo £ ❷ Hidden away amidst the hustle and bustle of HaCarmel Market is this decades-old hummus joint, where the hummus is made exactly the way it was 50 years ago. Ask any of the street vendors to point you in the right direction. ⓐ HaCarmel Market 🕐 08.00–14.30 Sun–Fri

Garden Café Sonia ££ ❸ This delightful café is a secret favourite with the locals, hidden down a side street off King George Street. The leafy tea garden with climbing plants and flowers is the perfect place to rest weary feet and enjoy a lunch from the extensive menu. ⓐ 1 Almonit Way ☎ 057 9442801 🕐 09.00–24.00 daily

Orna and Ella ££ ❹ Let the queues of people waiting for a table on Friday mornings attest to the popularity of this quintessentially Tel Avivian café-restaurant, located on trendy Sheinkin Street. The menu offers plenty of light meals and snacks, with lots of vegetarian options. ⓐ 33 Sheinkin St ☎ 03 6204753 🕐 10.00–24.00 Sun–Fri, 11.00–24.00 Sat

Tazza d'Oro ££ ❺ Located in Tel Aviv's oldest neighbourhood, Neve Tzedek, this café sums up the arty, bohemian vibe of the area. It has a lovely little patio which is packed with regulars on weekends, but quieter during the week. The coffee is imported from Italy and there is a menu of tasty lunches and snacks.
ⓐ 6 Ahad Haam St ⏰ 07.30–24.00 Sun–Thur, 07.30–01.00 Fri, 08.30–24.00 Sat

AFTER DARK

RESTAURANTS

Manta Ray £££ ❻ This laid-back beachfront restaurant specialises in fresh fish and seafood and offers a great selection of tasty Middle-Eastern food and mezze (small salad and side orders) for diners to select from. It's the perfect place to sit and indulge in the fruits of the sea, with waves lapping almost at your toes. ⓐ Alma Beach ☎ 03 5174773 ⓦ www.mantaray.co.il
⏰ 09.00–12.00, 12.30–24.00 daily

Max Brenner £££ ❼ This now international chain of restaurants has become something of an institution in Israel. While main courses are creative and incredibly tasty, they are simply a distraction from the wonderful desserts. For Max Brenner is a specialist in all things chocolatey, and the attached gift shop is a great place to pick up some sweet souvenirs.
ⓐ 45 Rothschild Blvd ☎ 03 5604570 ⓦ www.maxbrenner.com
⏰ 09.00–late Sun–Thur, 08.00–late Fri & Sat

BARS & NIGHTCLUBS

The Barbie The Barbie has long played host to top rock bands and singers visiting Tel Aviv, both home-grown and from abroad. The club is dark and crowded with youngsters enthusiastically dancing to the pumping tunes. ⓐ 40 Salame Rd ⓣ 03 5188123 ⓘ Admission charge varies with the performer

Levontine 7 The charismatic and bohemian Levontin neighbourhood is the setting for this funky bar that hosts regular live music events and attracts a chilled-out crowd. ⓐ 7 Levontin St ⓣ 03 5605084 ⓛ 19.00–late daily

Rothschild 12 While the décor is wooden and rustic, in the style of a French saloon, the clientele is anything but and this is one of the trendiest bars around. The location on fashionable Rothschild Boulevard and the extensive drinks list only add to its increasing popularity. ⓐ 12 Rothschild Blvd ⓣ 03 5106430 ⓛ 19.00–late Sat–Thur

Jaffa

Jaffa and Tel Aviv may be considered one city, but in many ways they couldn't be more opposite. Tel Aviv, at just 100 years old, is cosmopolitan, young and chiefly Jewish, while 4,000-year-old Jaffa is traditional, ancient and predominantly Arabic. The Old City lives up to every expectation of quaint, with its cobbled lanes, hodgepodge of stone buildings, picturesque fishing port and thriving artists' colony. Outside the historic centre Jaffa is a buzz of activity. Cars clamour through the narrow streets, bakeries and hummus joints churn out freshly made snacks and Arab culture prevails.

SIGHTS & ATTRACTIONS

Clock Tower
The three-storey-high Clock Tower, one of Jaffa's most recognisable features, is one of only seven clock towers built in Palestine during the Ottoman period. Interestingly, the clock was once set to European time so as not to confuse the seafaring merchants arriving at the port. A free guided tour leaves every Wednesday at 09.30 from Clock Tower Square.

HaPigsa Gardens
Within the Old City and located on the small hill that marks its highest point are these pretty gardens. While the landscaping is attractive enough, it is the spectacular view along the Tel Aviv-Jaffa coastline that has visitors reaching for their cameras. The vista is equally impressive by day,

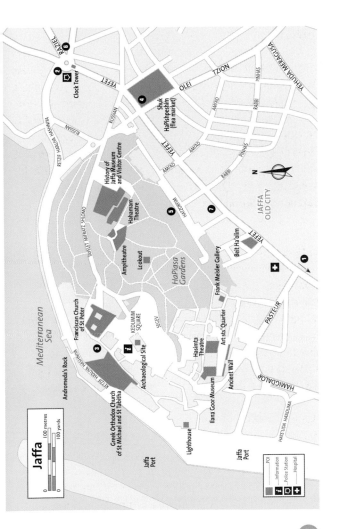

Jaffa

0   100 metres
0   100 yards

Mediterranean Sea

Andromeda's Rock

Greek Orthodox Church of St Michael and St Tabitha 3

Jaffa Port

Lighthouse

Jaffa Port

Franciscan Church of St Peter

Archaeological Site 2

KEDUMIM SQUARE

Ilana Goor Museum

Ancient Wall

Hasimta Theatre

Art sts' Quarter

Frank Meisler Gallery

Beit Ha'olim

HaPisga Gardens

Amphitheatre

Lookout

Hahamam Theatre

History of Jaffa Museum and Visitor Centre

TAYELET MIFRATZ SHLOMO

RETZIF HAALIYA HASHNIYA

RETZIF HAALIYA HASHNIYA

RUSSIAN

Clock Tower 2

RAZIEL 6

YEFET

RUSSIAN

RETZIF HAVIVA HASHNIYA

Shuk HaPishpeshim (flea market) 4

OLEI

TZION

YEHUDA MERAGUSA

AMIAD

RABBI

PINHAS

AMIAD

RABBI

PINHAS

YEFET

HATZORFIM

AMIAD

N

JAFFA OLD CITY

YEFET

PASTEUR

HATE'UDA HADUUMA

HAMIDGALOR

5

7

1

POI
Information
Police Station
Hospital

95

● *HaPigsa Gardens offer commanding views of the coast*

when the beaches are busy, the sun shining and the sky blue, as by night, when the city's lights twinkle alluringly. Within the gardens is a small amphitheatre where summer concerts are often held.

Kedumim Square & churches

The square sits at the centre of the Old City, with a maze of lanes leading down from it to the port, and HaPigsa Gardens leading up the small hill. Fringing the square are small restaurants, jewellery and craft shops and two large churches: the crumbling **Franciscan Church of St Peter** (🕐 08.00–11.45, 15.00–17.00 daily ❶ Modest dress required), said to have been visited by Napoleon, and the ornate **Greek Orthodox Church of St Michael and St Tabitha** (🕐 08.00–11.45, 15.00–17.00 daily ❶ Modest dress required).

Port & Andromeda's Rock

It is difficult to imagine as you wander around the tranquil port with its little fishing boats, piles of nets, warehouses containing art exhibits and fish restaurants that this was once one of the world's busiest seaports, but excavations and biblical texts have revealed a long and successful history. Just beyond the sea wall are several rocks, the darkest of which is said to be Andromeda's Rock. In Greek mythology the beautiful Andromeda was chained to this rock by her father King Cepheusas, as a sacrifice to Poseidon's sea monster. According to legend her brave hero came in the form of Perseus, who slew the monster. Today the port is a lovely place to explore, and while it isn't necessarily as beautiful as other parts of the Old City, the scents emanating from the small fish restaurants and its old-world atmosphere provide plenty of charm.

Flea market

The flea market, known also as Shuk HaPishpeshim, makes for a true Middle Eastern experience, with colourful items being haggled for amid busy chatter. Goods for sale vary from brass and copper to Persian tiles to Judaica. Second-hand clothes, textiles, antique furniture and decorative bits and pieces also all add to the general and seemingly disorganised mishmash of stalls. Perusing the mountains of items in search of a bargain has become a popular activity, especially on Fridays when the market is full to bursting and the surrounding cafés, restaurants and galleries teem with activity. The decades-old market has recently found itself at the centre of one of Tel Aviv's latest trends and is now one of the new 'in' drinking and socialising hangouts. ● 10.00–18.00 Sun–Thur, 10.00–14.00 Fri

CULTURE

Artists' Quarter

Leading down towards the port amid a labyrinth of cobbled lanes, old stone buildings and brightly coloured bougainvillea plants is Jaffa's burgeoning artists' quarter. Come here to peruse the workshops of both acclaimed and up-and-coming artists. While there are countless to explore, **Ilana Goor Museum** (● 4 Mazal Dagim St ● 03 6837676 ● www.ilanagoor.com ● 10.00–16.00 Tues–Fri & Sun, 10.00–18.00 Sat ● Admission charge) and **Frank Meisler Gallery** (● 25 Mazal Arie St

Kedumim Square is an interesting old site

⬤ *The atmospheric old Artists' Quarter*

① 03 5123000 ⓛ 09.00–23.00 Sun–Thur, 09.00–16.00 Fri, 18.00–23.00 Sat ① Admission charge) are of particular interest.

History of Jaffa Museum and Visitor Centre

The museum, which depicts the long and colourful history of the area, is also home to the Jaffa Visitor Centre. Reconstructions of tools and buildings have been placed within the excavated walls, which date to the Hellenistic and Roman periods, including life-sized figures. There is also an audio-visual presentation and exhibits of artefacts throughout the ages. ⓛ 10.00–18.00 daily ① Admission charge

TAKING A BREAK

In addition to those listed below, the cafés that surround the flea market are some of the best and most unique places to rest your feet. They transform from cafés during the day to bars at night, and several of the most popular are listed under 'Bars & nightclubs' (see page 103).

Abu Hassan (Ali Karavan) £ ❶ One of the city's longest-standing hummus joints, this simple eatery serves hummus – and hummus only – and generally stays open until the hummus runs out mid-afternoon. It is always busy and is great for a quick, delicious, cheap lunch. ⓐ 1 Dolphin St ① 03 6820387 ⓛ 07.45–14.45 Sun–Fri

Haj Kahil Shawarma £ ❷ For those who have had their fill of chickpeas, *shawarma* is a tasty, inexpensive alternative, and

there are few better places to try it than here. A steady stream of patrons means the slow-roasted lamb, turkey and beef doesn't sit there all day and is fresh and expertly cooked.
ⓐ Clock Tower Sq 🕐 09.00–24.00 daily

Napoleon Patisserie £ ❸ Israeli TV chef Nir Zook's latest venture looks to be as promising as his others (see opposite). Decadent, delicate cakes, sweet and savoury pastries, quiches and fresh orange juice make for the ideal mid-morning brunch, and the setting in an old stone Jaffa building is simple and enchanting.
ⓐ 15 Kedumim Sq ☎ 077 4030258 🕐 07.00–late daily

Said el Abu Lafia Bakery £ ❹ The bakery opened its doors in 1880 and remains one of the city's best-loved snack shops to this day. The smell of fresh baking wafts temptingly along the street, making it nigh on impossible to go by without stopping for a sample. Choose between a slice of Arabic-style pizza, warm, moist pittas, fluffy *burekas*, freshly baked breads and sticky baklava. ⓐ 7 Yefet St ☎ 03 6834958 🕐 08.00–22.00 Mon–Sat

AFTER DARK

RESTAURANTS
Noa Bistro ££ ❺ Noa's forms the more laid-back, affordable alternative to Cordelia Restaurant (see opposite), which is owned and run by the same chef. The meals are creative and unusual, and the menu is a mouthwatering combination of meats, fish and vegetable dishes. The hearty breakfast is a

particular highlight. ⓐ 14 Hatzorfim St ⓣ 03 5189720
ⓛ 09.30–late Sun–Thur daily

Yoe'ezer Wine Bar ££ ❻ Fine wines, rich cheese platters, and sumptuous dishes such as veal with truffles and fresh oysters, all served within the décor of a Crusader-era building make this a romantic choice within ancient Jaffa. ⓐ 2 Ish Habira St ⓣ 03 6839115 ⓛ 13.00–01.00 daily

Cordelia Restaurant £££ ❼ This Nir Zook creation is one of the city's most highly acclaimed gourmet restaurants. From the moment you step inside you know it will be a special evening – which is just as well, as it doesn't come cheap. The restaurant is housed within a Crusader-era building, the food is daring and creative French-style fusion and the ambience quiet and romantic. ⓐ 30 Yefet St ⓣ 03 5184668 ⓛ 12.30–15.30 & 19.00–24.00 Mon–Sat

BARS AND NIGHTCLUBS

Yaffa Bar A far cry from the overly fashionable wine bars of modern Tel Aviv is this cosy, comfortable watering hole, in the same complex as Cordelia Restaurant. Big sofas, indoor and outdoor seating, a broad selection of well-priced light meals and snacks and a relaxed atmosphere make it a good choice for a relaxed evening out. ⓐ 30 Yefet St ⓣ 03 5184668 ⓛ 20.00–late daily

The flea market has become the latest place for the more casual, bohemian and chilled-out set to spend an evening.

Daytime cafés cater also to evening punters and the charm of the market itself (open late on Thursdays) makes for a unique after-dark experience. There are many bar-cafés scattered around Jaffa that are worth ferreting out, but the following are three of the most popular:

Puah ⓐ 3 Rabbi Yohanan ⓣ 03 6823821 ⓛ 10.00–01.00 Sun–Wed, 24 hrs Thur–Sat

Shafa ⓐ 2 Nahman St ⓣ 03 6811205 ⓛ 17.00–02.00 Mon–Thur, 12.00–17.00 Fri

Sharkuteri ⓐ 3 Rabbi HaNina ⓣ 03 6828843 ⓛ 12.00–17.00 & 19.00–late Mon–Sat

◗ *The Dead Sea is an unmissable excursion*

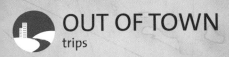

OUT OF TOWN
trips

Jerusalem

Although they are in many ways diametric opposites,
Jerusalem's capacity to entertain is by no means secondary
to that of fun-loving, secular Tel Aviv. Plus, of course, this
undeniably unique city is one of the world's most ancient,
intriguing and historically significant, and one that has been
battled over for centuries.

The Old City stands out as the highlight of any visit, and is
a maze of architectural antiquities, thriving religious
communities, busy souks and historical treasures. Outside the
Old City walls, neighbourhoods range from the traditional to
the ultra-Orthodox to the modern – an inimitable combination
that attracts throngs of visitors.

GETTING THERE

From Tel Aviv the easiest and quickest way to get to Jerusalem is
by bus. Bus 405 does the one-hour journey every 20 minutes
throughout the day (except on Shabbat, the Jewish sabbath)
and costs 20NIS. The bus departs from the central bus station,
stopping also at Merkaz station. In Jerusalem it takes you to the
central bus station on Jaffa Road, and from there you can easily
walk to many of the historic city-centre sights. Another option is
to jump on one of the buses heading towards the Old City or to
the museums.

The journey by train takes half an hour longer and stops at
Malha, a southern neighbourhood of Jerusalem, from where you
can get a connecting bus to the centre.

SIGHTS AND ATTRACTIONS

Old City

Few would argue that Jerusalem's Old City isn't one of the most breathtaking, fascinating and emotive places in the world. The 2.5 sq km (1 sq mile) walled city has seen its share of turmoil throughout its long and dramatic history, and has been conquered, attacked and razed to the ground many times over. For it is here that Judaism, Christianity and Islam meet, where a potpourri of religious buildings vie for space in the narrow cobbled alleys and clamorous souks, and where residents, traditionally robed religious folk and tourists wander side by side.

A huge wall encircles the Old City, containing several gates. The busiest are the Damascus and Jaffa gates, with the latter the most common entrance for visitors (the visitor centre is located just inside). The city is divided into four quarters inside the wall: Muslim, Christian, Jewish and Armenian. Each has its own distinct character and appeal, but it is often difficult to know where one ends and the next begins.

Western Wall

The Western Wall, or HaKotel, is the last remnant of the long-destroyed Second Temple that once stood here, and is the holiest site in Judaism. It is often referred to as the Wailing Wall because of the tears shed by Jews over the temple's destruction. Today, the Western Wall is an important pilgrimage site and centre of daily prayer (Jews place their prayers into the cracks in the walls). The wall is divided into two separate prayer sections for men and women. ❶ Modest dress required

Church of the Holy Sepulchre

The church stands as the most revered site in Christianity, as is attested by the throngs of pilgrims who pour through the doors. Built over the sites where tradition states Jesus' crucifixion, burial and resurrection occurred, it is a cavernous construction with a maze of ornately decorated corridors and chapels. The church holds a wealth of historically intriguing and ecclesiastically significant sites, from the **Unction Stone**, revered as the site where Jesus' body was laid out, to **Calvary (Golgotha)**, held to be where Jesus was crucified, to the **Rotunda**, worshipped as Jesus' tomb. 🕐 04.30–19.00 daily

⬤ The Western Wall is a sacred site for Jews

Temple Mount

The golden Dome of the Rock is an unmistakable landmark on the Jerusalem skyline, sitting in the midst of the Temple Mount complex. Considered the third-holiest site in Islam is the Al-Aqsa Mosque, believed to be from where Muhammad ascended to heaven. The site is also revered by Jews as the spot upon which the Foundation Stone – from where they believe the world was built – stands. It has therefore long been the centre of the turmoil that exists in the relationship between Jews and Muslims, and is the site of the destroyed First and Second temples. The Dome of the Rock and Al-Aqsa Mosque are closed to non-Muslims, but the complex itself is a wonderful and serene place to visit. Ensure you are dressed modestly, however, and abide by religious laws. ⓘ 02 6283292 ⏰ 07.30–10.00, 12.30–13.30 Sun–Thur

Via Dolorosa

The Via Dolorosa is a ceremonial walk through the Old City of Jerusalem that follows the route along which tradition states Jesus carried the cross to his crucifixion. The path begins in the far corner of the Muslim Quarter near the Omadiye Madrassa, which is believed to be the site where Pontius Pilate tried and convicted Jesus and from where the long walk to Golgotha began. The route leads through the Muslim and Christian quarters and is marked (often subtly) by plaques and small chapels, each known as a station of the cross. Leaflets sold by street vendors throughout the Old City will give details of each station. The Via Dolorosa ends inside the Church of the Holy Sepulchre (see page 109).

Me'a Shearim neighbourhood

One of Jerusalem's most intriguing neighbourhoods is ultra-Orthodox Me'a Shearim. It is undoubtedly a unique place – a kind of remnant of a bygone era where traditional Jewish dress is worn without exception, Yiddish not Hebrew is spoken and an atmosphere of religious learning permeates. Signs warn visitors to heed the religious laws, and it is inadvisable to enter during Shabbat hours. ❶ Modest dress is mandatory, including long skirts for women

⬤ View from the Mount of Olives across Jerusalem's Old City

CULTURE

Yad Vashem Holocaust Memorial Museum

Yad Vashem has become a site of remembrance for the six million Jews and countless others who lost their lives in one of the world's most terrible genocides. The museum complex is designed as a timeline of events leading up to and during the Holocaust, and displays are frank, moving and often chilling. A garden of remembrance provides a peaceful contrast to the museum. ⓐ Herzl Blvd ❶ 02 6443420 ⓦ www.yadvashem.org ⏱ 09.00–17.00 Sun–Wed, 09.00–20.00 Thur, 09.00–14.00 Fri ❶ Under 10s not allowed

Israel Museum

The Israel Museum houses some of the world's most impressive and historically significant exhibits and artefacts. The Dead Sea Scrolls are presented in their own wing, and other exhibits include Judaica from across the world, works by renowned artists, ethnographic displays and a vast and detailed model of Jerusalem's Second Temple. ⓐ Ruppin Rd ❶ 02 6708811 ⓦ www.imj.org.il ⏱ 10.00–17.00 Sat–Mon, Wed & Thur, 16.00–21.00 Tues, 10.00–14.00 Fri ❶ Admission charge

RETAIL THERAPY

Mahane Yehuda Market

The hustle and bustle, crowds, scents and tastes of Mahane Yehuda Market are one of the most authentic and entertaining experiences outside the Old City. The market sells everything from fresh fruit and vegetables, spices, olives, meats and fish to home items and clothes, and come Friday morning is jam-packed as residents prepare for Shabbat. Nestled among the countless stalls are numerous small, rustic eateries, whose Middle Eastern dishes and traditional home cooking place them easily among the best eating spots in the city. If you buy only one thing, make sure it's the sticky-sweet baklava. ⓐ Mahane Yehuda neighbourhood 🕓 09.00–20.00 Sun–Thur, 09.00–Shabbat Fri

🔺 *Jerusalem's historic Via Dolorosa*

TAKING A BREAK

Abu Shukri £ A cheap, simple hummus joint regarded as the best in Jerusalem. It is located in the Muslim Quarter souk – just look for the queues. ⓐ 63 Al Wad Rd ⓣ 02 6271538 ⓛ 08.30–18.00 daily

Viennese Café £ Perfectly located in the heart of the Muslim Quarter this delightful coffee shop and bakery is housed in the grand Austrian Hospice building. Be sure to go up on to the roof for a spectacular view over the Old City. ⓐ Austrian Hospice, 37 Via Dolorosa ⓣ 02 6265800 ⓛ 07.00–22.00 daily

Ima ££ Located near the bustling Mahane Yehuda Market, this kosher eatery serves hearty Jewish and Middle Eastern food. ⓐ 189 Agripas St ⓣ 02 6246860 ⓛ 11.00–23.00 Sun–Thur, 11.00–Shabbat Fri

Little Jerusalem Restaurant at Ticho House ££ The shady courtyard here makes for an ideal pit stop on a walking tour. Light vegetarian dishes are served and regular poetry and classical music recitals are held. ⓐ 9 Harav Kook St ⓣ 02 6244186 ⓛ 10.00–24.00 Sun–Thur, 09.00–15.00 Fri, end of Shabbat–24.00 Sat

AFTER DARK

RESTAURANTS
Armenian Tavern ££ Nestled in the quiet Armenian Quarter of the Old City, this is a unique dining experience where

Armenian dishes are served in an ancient, romantic cellar.
ⓐ 79 Armenian Orthodox Patriarchate St ⓣ 02 6273854
ⓛ 11.00–22.00 Mon–Sat

Blue Dolphin ££ This old East Jerusalem favourite serves fresh fish cooked in a Lebanese-Mediterranean style. ⓐ 7 Shimon HaTzadik St ⓣ 02 5322001 ⓛ 12.00–24.00 daily

Eucalyptus £££ Biblical foods have been created with unusual ingredients to produce an elegant, gourmet dining experience. ⓐ 14 Hativat Yerushalayim St ⓣ 02 6244331 ⓦ www.the-eucalyptus.com ⓛ 12.00–24.00 Sun–Thur, 10.00–Shabbat Fri, end of Shabbat–late Sat

Machaneyuda £££ The latest fad in the city, this funky restaurant has a creative menu that changes nearly every day.

THE DEAD SEA

The Dead Sea is one of the planet's most fascinating and unique geological phenomena and is located at its lowest point (400 m/1,312 ft) below sea level. Day trips from Jerusalem are highly recommended and easily made. Buses 486, 421 and 487 make the 1-hour-and-20-minute journey to the shore of the Dead Sea in the barren beauty of the Judean Desert every two hours. Float in the extremely salty waters, visit a health spa at Ein Bokek, climb to the top of Masada or hike through the Ein Gedi National Park oasis.

📍 10 Beit Yaakov St 📞 02 5333442 🕐 18.30–late Sun–Thur,
12.00–18.00 Fri, 21.00–late Sat

BARS

Cellar Bar This refined, relaxed bar is located in the beautiful,
historic American Colony Hotel and is a big favourite with
visiting diplomats and foreign journalists. 📍 23 Nablus Rd
📞 02 6279777 🕐 19.00–24.00 daily

Constantine A big, lively bar/club that has regular live music
performances, themed nights and modern, flashy decor.
📍 3 Hahistadrut St 📞 02 6221155 🕐 21.00–late daily

Egon A bohemian-style pub with cosy floor cushions and a
relaxed vibe. 📍 9 Nahalat Shiva St 📞 02 6222458 🕐 24 hrs daily

THEATRE & FILM

Khan Theatre Israeli and Hebrew plays, classical concerts and
folklore performances. 📍 2 David Remez Sq 📞 02 6718281
🌐 www.khan.co.il

Jerusalem Cinematheque Shows classical, avant-garde,
Hollywood and experimental films in Hebrew and English.
📍 11 Hebron Rd 📞 02 6724131 🌐 www.jer-cine.org.il

ACCOMMODATION

Abraham Hostel £ An excellent new hostel, catering to
independent budget travellers. Private rooms and dorms are

available, and kitchen use, free breakfast, a travel centre, games room and Wi-Fi are all included. ⓐ 67 Hanevi-im St ⓣ 02 6502200 ⓦ www.abrahamhostels.com ⓔ reservations@abrahamhostels.com

Gloria Hotel ££ An excellent Old City hotel, housed in an old stone mansion and located by Jaffa Gate. The spacious rooms have AC and TV and there is a bar and restaurant. ⓐ 33 Latin Patriarchate St ⓣ 02 6282431/2 ⓦ www.gloria-hotel.com ⓔ gloriahl@netvision.net.il

Knight's Palace ££ A beautiful stone building on a peaceful alley with flagstone floors, arched windows and vaulted ceilings, elegant bedrooms, views over the Old City, and a bar and restaurant. ⓐ Freres St ⓣ 02 6282537 ⓦ www.knightspalace.com ⓔ kp@actcom.co.il

Park Hotel ££ The sunny, spacious rooms in this hotel come with all mod cons and offer excellent value for money. Breakfast is served on the covered patio and there is Wi-Fi throughout. ⓐ 2 Vilnay St ⓣ 02 6582222 ⓦ www.park-hotel-jerusalem.com ⓔ reservation@park-hotel-jerusalem.com

King David £££ Before becoming the country's most famous and elegant place to stay, this hotel offered asylum to exiled monarchs, was headquarters of the British Mandate authorities and was bombed by a Zionist militant group in 1946. ⓐ 23 King David St ⓣ 02 6208888 ⓦ www.danhotels.com ⓔ kingdavid@danhotels.com

Akko

Heading north out of Tel Aviv, Israel's Mediterranean coast stretches for miles. Along this shore are some of the country's most beautiful, wild beaches, impressive archaeological ruins, historic cities and the rolling Mount Carmel range. Akko itself is enchanting. Stout old city walls surround a hodgepodge of ancient buildings, many of which date from the Crusader period. Minaret towers reach into the sky, a busy, aromatic souk snakes its way through the city's heart and layers of historical intrigue are woven into the living Arab city, its cobbled lanes and busy fishing port.

GETTING THERE

Buses make the long and indirect journey several times a day from Tel Aviv, but by far the quickest and most convenient way to get to Akko is by train. Trains do the journey in 1 hour 30 minutes, and take only 55 minutes to reach nearby Haifa. The train and bus stations are in Akko's new city but taxis can take you to the visitor centre. If renting a car is within your budget then it can be a lovely addition to a trip, allowing you to stop at Haifa and the Caesarea Maritime National Park (see page 126) along the way.

SIGHTS & ATTRACTIONS

Municipal Museum

Akko's baths were built by the Ottoman ruler Ahmed Al-Jazzar as part of his grand mosque complex and were designed in the

◯ *Al-Jazzar Mosque in Akko's Old City*

style of Roman bath houses, with different rooms of varying heat. Today they form a unique museum experience with ancient statues, lights, sounds and an interesting tour by a holographic bath attendant. ❶ 04 9551088 ❷ 08.30–17.00 Sat–Thur, 08.30–14.00 Fri (winter), 08.30–18.00 Sat–Thur, 08.30–17.00 Fri (summer) ❸ Admission charge

Al-Jazzar Mosque

The iconic blue mosque that stands in the entrance to the Old City is the largest mosque in the country outside of Jerusalem. It was built by the Ottoman ruler Al-Jazzar in 1781 and is an important site of prayer. The mosque houses not only the sarcophagi of Al-Jazzar but also what are claimed to be hairs from the Prophet Muhammad. The hairs are put on display once a year at the end of Ramadan. ❶ 04 991303 ❷ 08.00–18.00 Sat–Thur, 08.00–11.00 & 13.00–18.00 Fri ❸ Admission charge; modest dress required

Citadel and Underground Prisoners Museum

Looming over the Underground Crusader City below is the citadel, built by Al-Jazzar during his rule of Akko. It was also during Al-Jazzar's rule that the Baha'i Faith's founder, Baha'u'llah was imprisoned in the citadel, and today his cell is open to visitors.

The British Mandate period in Palestine saw the citadel transformed into government buildings and the country's largest prison, housing Jewish Zionist underground fighters. Famous stories from these tumultuous years of resistance include the attempted escape by members of a Jewish militant

⬥ The Knights' Hall in the huge Underground Crusader City

121

group who broke into the citadel to free the prisoners. Despite failure, it was seen an important step for Jewish freedom fighters in weakening British control, and the prison is today the Underground Prisoners Museum. The noose from which Jewish resistance fighters were hanged is on display alongside photographs and documents. ❶ 04 9918264 ❷ 09.00–17.00 Sun–Thur, 09.00–13.00 Fri ❸ Admission charge

Underground Crusader City

Akko's phases of occupation are nowhere more obvious than in the Underground Crusader City. When the Crusaders arrived here, Akko had been a thriving port city for centuries and the Knights Hospitaller made it their capital in the Holy Land. The enormous fortress that they built here formed the heart of their capital, but was abandoned when the Crusaders were defeated and subsequently buried under later fortifications. Extensive excavations that began in 1950 have revealed a series of vast, gothic halls and rooms, each with high, vaulted ceilings, big windows and ornate columns. The most impressive are those which served as a ceremonial and dining hall for the knights. ❶ 04 9956706 ❷ 08.30–18.00 Sat–Thur, 08.30–17.00 Fri (summer), 08.30–17.00 Sat–Thur, 08.30–16.00 Fri (winter) ❸ Admission charge

RETAIL THERAPY

Souk

A long colourful souk weaves its way through the heart of the Old City, shoehorned into the cobbled lanes in between churches, mosques and *khans* (ancient merchants' inns). It is a lively, noisy place where residents buy fresh produce and household items, and tourists enjoy the traditional wares. Everything can be found in the souk from baklava, fresh fruit juices, dried fruit, nuts, spices, hummus and olives, to butchers shops, bakeries, and glass *nargilah* pipes.

TAKING A BREAK

Humus Saeid £ One of the most famous hummus joints in the country, Humus Saeid is snuggled into the heart of the souk, and can most easily be found by the queues outside. Needless to say, this isn't a lunch to lounge over but no trip to Akko would be complete without a visit. ⓐ Souk ⓣ 04 9913945 ⓛ 06.00–until food runs out (usually around 14.30) Sun–Fri

Misedet HaDayagim (The Fisherman's Restaurant) ££ Tucked into a corner of the harbour entrance is this rustic little Arabic-style eatery that serves fried fish and a big selection of salads. First go into the fishmonger next door, choose your fish and then head into the tiny restaurant where they will cook it on the spot. ⓐ Harbour entrance ⓣ 04 9911985 ⓛ 12.00–19.00 daily

AFTER DARK

RESTAURANTS
Abu Christo £££ If the menu doesn't bowl you over, the view from the top of the ramparts will. This well-loved restaurant has been around for years and has not lost any of its pizzazz. Greek-

and Arabic-style salads, fresh seafood and succulent steaks are elegantly presented and expertly cooked. ⓐ South Sea Prom ⓣ 04 9910065 ⓦ www.abu-christo.co.il ⓛ 12.00–23.00 daily

Uri Buri £££ Boasting another prime location near the lighthouse is Uri Buri, famed throughout Israel for its outstanding fish and seafood dishes. While the décor is informal yet classy, the prices are high and this is a real 'treat yourself' experience. ⓐ HaHaganah St ⓣ 04 9552212 ⓦ www.uriburi.co.il ⓛ 12.00–24.00 daily

ACCOMMODATION

Akko Gate Hostel £ This family-run hostel and guesthouse offers an ideal location just outside the Old City main entrance and is great value for money. The rooms are clean and tidy – those in the newer wing are more spacious and modern – and there is a small café on-site and free Wi-Fi. Dormitory accommodation is also available. ⓐ 14 Saladin St ⓣ 04 9910410 ⓦ www.akkogate.com ⓔ walid.akko.gate@gmail.com

Zipi's Place ££ A 20-minute walk or 5-minute taxi ride from the Old City, Zipi's is a cosy, family-run guesthouse offering private rooms and dormitory beds. Wi-Fi, a communal kitchen and laundry facilities are also available. ⓐ 10 Bilu St ⓣ 04 9915220 ⓔ zipi503@walla.com

Akkotel £££ This elegant boutique hotel has been built into the Old City walls and is steeped in traditional architectural and decorative features. The rooms are spacious and well equipped, and there is a wonderful rooftop café and a Mediterranean fish restaurant. ⓐ Saladin St ⓣ 04 9877100 ⓦ www.akkotel.com ⓔ info@akkotel.com

◆ *The ancient Roman ruins of Caesarea*

ON THE WAY TO AKKO

Baha'i Shrine, Haifa Without exception, any tourism photo of Haifa will display the immaculate, colourful gardens that tumble down through the city centre to the picturesque German colony. In their centre sits the golden Baha'i Shrine and together they make an impressive sight. The Baha'i Faith has made this its headquarters, and the shrine is the final resting place of Bab, founder of the Faith. Free tours are offered (daily except Wednesday) and the site is UNESCO World Heritage listed. ⓐ Haifa ☎ 04 8313131 🕐 09.00–17.00 daily

Caesarea Maritime National Park Once one of the world's largest port cities is today an impressive archaeological site. Caesarea's history is long and fascinating. It played a crucial role in the Byzantine period, and also during Roman rule under King Herod. It saw Vespasian declared Emperor, Paul the Apostle's trial and was the home of Pontius Pilate. The great hippodrome and theatre owe their origins to this time, as does the submerged port. The later Crusader city became a heavily fortified stronghold in the Holy Land and many of its stout defences date to this time. ⓐ About halfway between Tel Aviv and Haifa, on the edge of the Caesarea ☎ 04 6267080 🌐 www.caesarea.com 🕐 08.00–18.00 Sun–Thur, 08.00–16.00 Fri (Apr–Sept); 08.00–16.00 Sun–Thur, 08.00–15.00 Fri (Oct–Mar) ❶ Admission charge

▶ *Trains offer a comfortable way of getting in and out of the city*

PRACTICAL
information

Directory

GETTING THERE

By air

Almost all visitors to Israel enter the country through Tel Aviv's Ben Gurion International Airport, which is served by major airlines from across the world as well as several budget airlines from Europe. In addition, some summer charter flights go to Eilat International Airport in the south of the country. The following fly or connect to Tel Aviv from the UK:

Air Berlin ☎ +49 30 41 02 10 03 ⓦ www.airberlin.com

British Airways ☎ 0844 493 0787 ⓦ www.ba.com

easyJet ⓦ www.easyjet.com

El Al ☎ +972 3 9716854 ⓦ www.elal.co.il

Israir ☎ +972 3 7954038 ⓦ www.israirairlines.com

Jet2 ☎ 0871 226 1737 ⓦ www.jet2.com

Many people are aware that air travel emits CO_2, which contributes to climate change. You may be interested in the possibility of lessening the environmental impact of your flight through the charity **Climate Care** (ⓦ www.jpmorgan climatecare.com), which offsets your CO_2 by funding environmental projects around the world.

By land

Israel has three border crossings with Jordan. Visas can usually be obtained at the border, with the exception of the King Hussein/Allenby Crossing; those wishing to cross there need to apply for a visa in advance from the Jordanian embassy in Tel Aviv.

Yitzhak Rabin/Arava Border Crossing This is used mainly for day trips to Petra and Wadi Rum in Jordan. Exit tax is 101NIS and a two-week Jordanian visa costs 20 dinars (£18). ⓐ Eilat ⓣ 08 6300555 ⓞ 06.30–20.00 Sun–Thur, 08.00–20.00 Fri & Sat

Allenby Border Crossing/King Hussein Bridge This border is used mainly for traffic between the Jordanian capital Amman and Jerusalem. Exit tax is 167NIS. ⓣ 02 5482600 ⓞ 08.00–20.00 Sun–Thur, 08.00–15.00 Fri & Sat

▲ *The clean and modern Ben Gurion Airport serves Tel Aviv*

Jordan River Crossing This is the northernmost border between the two countries. Exit tax is 101NIS and two-week Jordanian visas are issued on the border for 20 dinars (£18). **a** Beit She'an **ⓘ** 04 6093400 **ⓒ** 08.00–21.00 Sun–Thur, 08.00–20.00 Fri & Sat

There is also one border crossing open to tourists between Israel and Egypt, which is modern, efficient and sees a steady stream of foreigners going in both directions.

Taba Border Crossing To travel to Sinai you don't need to apply for a visa in advance but can obtain one at the crossing for 46 Egyptian pounds (£5). There is a 101NIS exit fee from Israel. If you plan on continuing to the Egyptian mainland you will need to apply for a visa at the Egyptian consulates in Tel Aviv or Eilat. **ⓘ** 08 6360999 **ⓒ** 24 hrs daily

By sea
There are no longer any ferries to or from Israel, but almost all major cruise lines offer trips that can include Israel on their itineraries. Cruise ships dock in Haifa's port.

ENTRY FORMALITIES
The stigma of having an Israeli stamp in your passport has plagued travellers for years, with many of the Arab nations who do not have diplomatic relations with the country refusing you entry. This used to mean a new and costly passport, but it is now possible to use a 17L form, which can be stamped in lieu of your passport. Simply ask immigration officers for a form on your arrival at Ben Gurion Airport – they won't offer it otherwise.

Citizens of the UK, USA, Canada, Australia, New Zealand and South Africa do not need visas to enter Israel for up to three months, although they must be in possession of a passport valid for six months from the date of entry.

In terms of customs, visitors may bring one litre of spirits, two litres of wine and 250g of tobacco into Israel but no raw meats or plants. Duty free is big business in Israel because of high tax on many electrical items – it is even possible to buy televisions and vacuum cleaners in duty free.

MONEY

Israel's currency is the New Israeli Shekel (NIS), referred to commonly as shekel (singular) or shkalim (plural). There are 100 agorot in one shekel, and there are 5, 10 and 50 agorot coins (singular: agora), and 1NIS, 5NIS and 10NIS coins. Bank notes come in denominations of 20, 50, 100 and 200 NIS. Standard exchange rates are usually around 5.8NIS to £1 and 3.6NIS to US$1 – at least at the time of writing. Visitors can

INSURANCE

Israel has a high standard of health care but it comes at a cost and therefore travel insurance is a must. Most policies do not cover against acts of terrorism, and while the chances of being involved in an attack are extremely slim, for your peace of mind you may want to check the small print. Dental care in the country is also hugely costly so ensure a policy covers at least emergency cover.

bring unlimited sums of money into the country, and foreign currency and traveller's cheques can be easily cashed at the airport, exchange bureaux found throughout the city, banks, post offices and most hotels. ATMs are commonplace and all international credit and debit cards are accepted. To exchange traveller's cheques you will need to show your passport and – as exchange rates vary – it's worth shopping around, especially if you're exchanging large sums. US dollars are widely accepted, especially in tourist centres and hotels. It is also worth noting that banks and post offices are closed on Shabbat so plan to change money before the weekend (although ATMs, and often exchange bureaux, will still be open).

TIPPING & BARGAINING

It is customary to tip 12 per cent in restaurants and cafés and Israelis tend to tip generously even if the service wasn't good (although this is not compulsory). Tipping in bars is appreciated but not expected, and it is the norm to round up to the nearest shekel in taxis (even though they may ask for more). Bargaining and haggling is done only in open markets.

HEALTH, SAFETY & CRIME

Israel is a modern, developed country with Western standards of health, hygiene and medical facilities. There are no required vaccinations to enter the country, although it is recommended to be up to date on tetanus, polio, rubella, mumps and diphtheria. Tap water is safe to drink – though visitors often find the chlorine taste unpalatable – and bottled water is cheap and widely available. The main health risks in Tel Aviv relate to heat; summer temperatures can reach in excess of 35°C (95°F) with intense humidity. Be sure to drink plenty of fluids and stay out of the full impact of the midday sun (Israelis love their air conditioning and it is easy to see why). Stray cats roam the streets in their thousands and while rabies is present in Israel, it is rare in the cities. However, if you are bitten by an animal see a doctor immediately.

Despite how it may sometimes be portrayed on the news, Israel is safe to visit. Crime levels in Tel Aviv are relatively low compared to those in many Western countries, and non-violent theft tends to be the biggest problem encountered by visitors. Terrorism is a fact of life in Israel, but security is high and attacks have decreased over the past few years. Check with your country's foreign office before travelling for up-to-date information.

OPENING HOURS

The standard working week in Israel is from Sunday to Thursday, but many service businesses (not usually offices) are open until early afternoon on Friday. Shabbat (the Sabbath) is from sunset on Friday to sunset on Saturday, and public transport does not run during this time. Shops, public transport and many other businesses will reopen after Shabbat ends (Saturday evening), which can seem quite unusual to visitors. In secular cities such as Tel Aviv restaurants and bars stay open throughout Shabbat. Normal opening hours are from 09.00 to 18.00, although shopping centres will stay open later. Post offices and banks are closed on Wednesday afternoons, and tourist attractions such as museums generally either close on Shabbat or have shorter Friday and Saturday hours.

TOILETS

Public toilets are Western-style, generally clean and of a good standard. They can be found in shopping centres, bus, train and petrol stations, on public beaches and in some town centres. Usually only the ones in bus stations charge a fee, which is around 1NIS. There are two flushes, a small one and a large one, so be careful not to waste water – the country is seriously lacking in it.

CHILDREN

Israelis love children and the phrase 'no children allowed' is seldom encountered. Tel Aviv is awash with child-friendly attractions from the Mamadion Water Park and everything else on offer at HaYarkon Park (see page 62) to Gordon and Frishman beaches (see page 58) and Gordon Swimming Pool (see page 33). Play areas can be found along the seafront, in parks and along the boulevards, and there are excellent playgroups and creches catering to parents as much as their offspring. All pharmacies stock international brands of nappies, food and pharmaceutical products.

In addition to the above, the following are great for keeping children entertained.

Diada Diada offers a jamboree of activities for young babies and parents. There are classes, an activity room, a café and a shop.
ⓐ 75 Ben Gurion Av ⓣ 03 5244484

Mini Israel Park Visitors feel like Gulliver in the Holy Land as they wander through reconstructions of the country's main religious, architectural and geographical structures. ⓐ Route 1, on the way to Jerusalem near Latrun ⓘ 08 9130000/10 ⓦ www.minisrael.co.il ⓛ 10.00–22.00 Sat–Thur (summer); 10.00–17.00 Sat–Thur, 10.00–14.00 Fri (winter) ⓘ Admission charge

Tel Aviv-Ramat Gan Safari Park Big family favourite that offers car or bus transport through the safari park and a walk-around zoo. A big green park outside the safari park is a top family barbecue spot at weekends. ⓐ Ramat Gan ⓘ 03 6305325 ⓦ www.safari.co.il ⓛ 09.00–19.00 Sun–Thur, 09.00–14.00 Fri ⓘ Admission charge

COMMUNICATIONS
Telephone

Israel has more mobile phones per capita than any other country in the world and connections are excellent, even in rural areas. All hotels have direct-dial phones, but these can be extremely pricey. A better option is to head to a newsagent's, either to buy a phone-booth calling card or, if they have one, to use the coin-operated phone on the counter. It is possible to rent mobile phones or SIM cards from several companies whose offices can be found in Ben Gurion Airport, but be sure to check the small print as the tariffs can be high, even for incoming calls. Most phone numbers include an area code (03 for Tel Aviv, 02 for Jerusalem and 04 for Haifa) but there is also a smaller telephone company that issues numbers that don't require a code.

Post

Post offices can be found throughout the country and are denoted by their red-and-white sign displaying a gazelle. Although branches differ slightly, most are open 08.00–12.00 and 15.30–18.30 on Sundays, Tuesdays and Thursdays, 08.30–12.30 on Wednesdays and 08.00–12.00 on Fridays. Postal services include registered mail, express and EMS (an international service) as well as poste restante. FedEx and DHL also have offices in Israel.

Internet

The Internet is big business in Israel and you don't have to look far to find free Wi-Fi. Internet cafés offer high-speed Internet, good facilities and reasonable prices.

ELECTRICITY

Power supply is 220V and while plug sockets take type-H three-pin plugs, which are unique to Israel, two-pin European ones will also work.

TRAVELLERS WITH DISABILITIES

Israel is well geared towards travellers with disabilities. Public transport, hotels, restaurants, museums and many national parks are wheelchair accessible and have disabled facilities. **Access Israel** (ⓦ www.aisrael.org) can provide more detailed information.

TOURIST INFORMATION

Tel Aviv's municipality is strongly embracing the tourism boom and facilities for visitors are plentiful. The main **tourist**

information centre can be found at 🅐 Tel Aviv Prom, 46 Herbert Samuel St (corner of 2 Geula St) 📞 03 5166188 🅦 www.visit-tlv.com 🅔 tamia@tourism.gov.il 🕓 09.30–17.00 Sun–Thur, 09.30–13.00 Fri. In addition to this, a new tourist office with a gift shop has recently opened at 🅐 96 Ben Yehuda St 📞 03 5299569 🕓 09.00–20.00 Sun–Thur, 09.00–14.00 Fri, 19.00–22.00 Sat.

There is also a **Mobile Segway Information Center** that operates in major tourist areas daily during July, August and September, from 13.00 to 19.00.

🔺 *The new tourist office on Ben Yehuda Street*

Emergencies

EMERGENCY NUMBERS

Israel has different numbers for different emergency services:

Police t 100

Ambulance t 101

Fire t 102

In Tel Aviv, the main police stations are located at a 221 Dizengoff St t 03 5454210 and a 14 HaRakevet St t 03 5644458. The **tourist police office**, where they generally speak better English, is located on the corner of Herbert Samuel St and Ge'ula St t 03 5165382.

MEDICAL SERVICES

English is widely spoken in all hospitals in Israel. The main hospital in Tel Aviv is **Ichilov Hospital**. a 6 Weizmann St t 03 6974444

Assuta Hospital Israel's largest private hospital. a 58–60 Jabotinsky St t 03 5201515

Superpharm Central branch of a nationwide chain of chemists. a Ground floor, Dizengoff Center t 03 6203798 ◷ 09.30–22.00 Sun–Thur, 09.00–15.30 Fri, 06.30–23.00 Sat

EMBASSIES & CONSULATES

Australia a Discount Bank Tower, Level 28, 23 Yehuda Halevi St t 03 6935000 w www.australianembassy.org.il

telaviv.embassy@dfat.gov.au 🕒 08.00–12.30, 13.00–16.30 Mon–Thur, 08.00–13.00 Fri

Canada @ Hasapanut Hse, 3–5 Nirim St ☎ 03 6363300 🌐 www.canadainternational.gc.ca/israel @ taviv@ international.gc.ca 🕒 08.00–16.30 Mon–Thur, 08.00–13.30 Fri

Republic of Ireland @ 3 Daniel Frisch St ☎ 03 6964166 🕒 08.00–13.00, 14.00–16.00 Mon–Thur, 08.00–13.00 Fri

South Africa @ Sason Hogi Tower, 17th Floor, 12a Abba Hillel St, Ramat Gan ☎ 03 5252566 🌐 www.safis.co.il @ diplomatie@ ambafrance-il.org 🕒 09.00–11.30 Mon, Tues, Thur & Fri, 09.00–11.30, 14.00–15.00 Wed

United Kingdom @ 192 HaYarkon St ☎ 03 7251222 🕒 08.00–16.00 Mon–Thur, 08.00–13.30 Fri
Consulate @ 1 Ben Yehuda St ☎ 03 5100166 🌐 ukinisrael.fco.gov.uk/en 🕒 08.00–13.00 Mon–Thur, 08.00–12.30 Fri

United States @ 71 HaYarkon St ☎ 03 5197575 🕒 08.00–16.00 Mon–Thur, 08.00–13.00 Fri
Consulate @ 1 Ben Yehuda St ☎ 03 5175151 🌐 www.telaviv.usembassy.gov 🕒 08.00–16.30 Mon–Fri

INDEX

ACKNOWLEDGEMENTS
Thomas Cook Publishing wishes to thank the photographers, picture libraries and other organisations, to whom the copyright belongs, for the photographs in this book.

Mark Bassett, pages 5, 21, 29, 43, 52, 57, 61, 64, 72, 83, 84, 87, 96, 99, 100, 105, 109, 113, 119, 121; Dreamstime, pages 9 (Amilevin), 13 (Slidezero), 37 (Paulprescott); Allison Gosney, pages 7, 16, 23, 26, 30, 32, 38, 47, 55, 127, 129, 137; Israel Government Tourist Office, pages 19, 40–41, 45, 63, 69, 81, 89, 111, 125; iTravelJerusalem, page 15.

For CAMBRIDGE PUBLISHING MANAGEMENT LIMITED:
Project editor: Ed Robinson
Copy editor: Kate Taylor
Layout: Trevor Double
Proofreaders: Nick Newton & Michele Greenbank
Indexer: Marie Lorimer

Send your thoughts to
books@thomascook.com

- Found a great bar, club, shop or must-see sight that we don't feature?
- Like to tip us off about any information that needs a little updating?
- Want to tell us what you love about this handy little guidebook and more importantly how we can make it even handier?

Then here's your chance to tell all! Send us ideas, discoveries and recommendations today and then look out for your valuable input in the next edition of this title.

Email the above address (stating the title) or write to:
pocket guides Series Editor, Thomas Cook Publishing, PO Box 227, Coningsby Road, Peterborough PE3 8SB, UK.

WHAT'S IN YOUR GUIDEBOOK?

Independent authors Impartial up-to-date information from our travel experts who meticulously source local knowledge.

Experience Thomas Cook's 165 years in the travel industry and guidebook publishing enriches every word with expertise you can trust.

Travel know-how Thomas Cook has thousands of staff working around the globe, all living and breathing travel.

Editors Travel-publishing professionals, pulling everything together to craft a perfect blend of words, pictures, maps and design.

You, the traveller We deliver a practical, no-nonsense approach to information, geared to how you really use it.

ABOUT THE AUTHOR

Samantha Wilson is a freelance travel writer and member of the British Guild of Travel Writers. She specialises in Israel and Latin American destinations as well as budget travel topics, and has written seven books and numerous magazine articles for worldwide publications. Samantha spent two years living in Tel Aviv and makes regular trips back for research, leisure and the hummus.